High Road To Tibet

Travels in China, Tibet, Nepal and India

John Dwyer

Cover design by Antoine Cutayar @ www.cutayar.com

ISBN   978-1-4452-4614-7

To contact the author or comment on any content in this book, visit http://www.highroadtotibet.com

Published by lulu.com

To Caroline

Preface

On my fourteenth birthday, my mother gave me a colour atlas of the world as a birthday gift. Little did she suspect the effect it would have on me. From the moment I opened its pages, I was spellbound. Each page contained detailed maps of far-away countries as well as photographs of strange and exotic-looking people. I leafed through each page in reverential silence, staring with fascination at each country and continent detailed there. However, it was Asia that interested me the most. A map of the vast continent was displayed across two pages and blurb descriptions shot out from its major attractions. Iconic symbols such as the Great Wall of China, the Taj Mahal, and the Terracotta Army were all there. I studied the pictures and tried to imagine what it would be like to be actually there.

I was also fascinated by the large blank spaces between each city. Did anyone live there, I wondered? I imagined that there must be some undiscovered mysteries in those empty areas. I went to bed that night, determined that I was going to visit those places one day and see for myself what they were really like.

This book is about the realisation of that dream.

Acknowledgements

There are many people I'd like to thank for their help in making this book a reality. The following people especially deserve a special mention for the assistance they provided. Stephen Warner edited every chapter of the book and gave me plenty of pointers on where things could be improved. Paul Clements provided professional help and advice when needed. Sue Booth-Forbes aided me with some very helpful and instructive advice from a creative point of view. Thanks so much to you all for your help.

I'd also like to thank the following people for volunteering to review chapters of the book and for providing their valued feedback – John Lynch, John Gilligan, David Nolan, Ed Roche-Kelly, Tina ManWarren Roche-Kelly, Mike Gallagher, Ed Valentine, William McSweeney, Denise Johnson, Philip O'Reilly, Kieran Harrington, Gerard Harrington, Shane McElwee, Paul O'Mahony, Tony Murphy, Jessica Murphy, Paul Whiting, David Herbert, Noel Phylan, Dominic Taylor, Peter Doran, Eoin Canny, Karen Minich, Stephen Meehan, and Brian McEvoy.

Finally, a big thanks to my wife Caroline. Without her understanding, help, and patience, this book would have been a much harder project to complete.

Section Dividers

As you read through each chapter, you will see section dividers that look like this:

ॐੴ

This divider is a slightly elongated mirror image of the ancient Om symbol, a sacred symbol that is recognised and revered by Buddhists and Hindus across China, Tibet, Nepal, and India. Since this is a character that is familiar in all the countries I traveled through, I decided to use it throughout the book and on my web site.

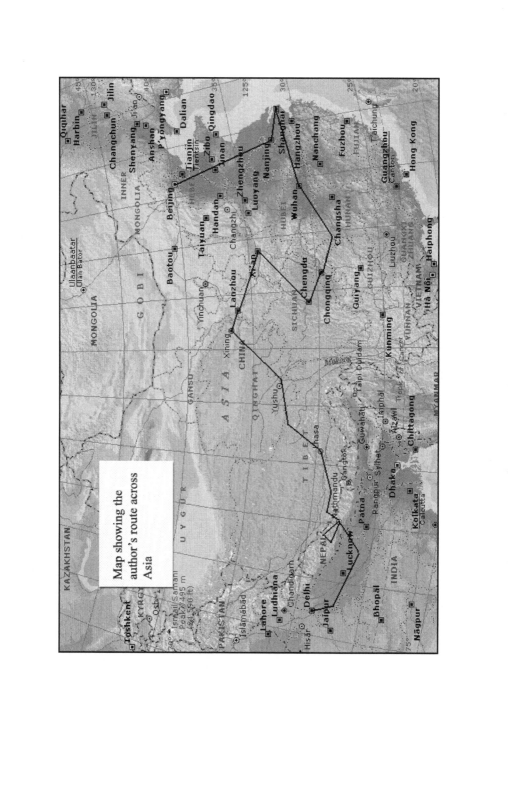

Map showing the author's route across Asia

Contents

1

ENTER THE DRAGON

"Please sir, may I make photo with you?" The voice sounded nervous. I turned to see a young woman holding a camera towards me, smiling brightly. I nodded my consent. She turned and beckoned to some individuals in the crowd. Two elderly people wearing matching blue baseball caps shuffled over and took up their positions on either side of me. I smiled and greeted them. They both wore grim expressions as we posed for the photograph. I put my arms around their shoulders and drew them closer. I remember how thin and bony the old man felt underneath his loose grey suit. The young woman composed her picture and clicked the shutter.

"Thank you, thank you," she said as she left with the elderly couple. The old man stopped briefly to wave at me but he had turned away again before I could wave back. I watched them until they melted into the crowds of Beijing's Tiananmen Square.

There was a festive atmosphere in the immense plaza of Tiananmen as people celebrated the end of the weeklong October National Holiday. Young children squealed with joy from

The Great Wall of China

A Chinese soldier under the portrait of Chairman Mao

the lofty heights of their fathers shoulders. Extended families enjoyed huge picnics on the ground. Young couples walked hand in hand while eating candyfloss. Vendors were doing a brisk trade in sweets and cold drinks. Everyone seemed to be having a good time and so was I.

I walked around and admired some of the displays that celebrated Chinese history and recent achievements. A leafy replica of the Great Wall ran along one side of the square. Nearby, a beautifully sculpted green pagoda tower rose majestically from an explosion of colourful flowers and shrubs. On another platform, a replica rocket marked the first Chinese astronaut in space. I looked around and smiled. Beijing was the starting point of a journey across Asia that I had been planning for months. I was giddy with excitement at the thoughts of the road ahead. What strange and exotic people would I meet? What adventures and sights would I enjoy? I couldn't wait to get started.

I left Tiananmen Square and wandered the short distance towards my hotel in the ancient Hutong area of the city. The Hutongs are a maze of labyrinthine laneways and alleys that once made up old Beijing. The narrow lanes bustled with business and commerce. I picked my way through the Hutong slowly, sidestepping cyclists and vendors on the busy thoroughfare. The smell of sweet potatoes and ears of corn roasting on hot coals filled the air. Restaurants, bicycle shops, and clothing stores all competed vigorously for business. Everyone seemed to be running a small enterprise. With all this capitalism, I had to remind myself that China was supposed to be a communist country.

While the rest of old Beijing was falling to the wrecking ball of development, life in the remaining Hutongs carried on as it had for centuries. Outside an ancient-looking doorway, a couple of old men were playing Chinese chess on an upturned wooden crate. A bowl of steaming tea rested beside each player. The game is similar to chess but the pieces are flat. It was a very popular board game in Beijing as I saw it played many times in the streets of the city during my visit. Down another laneway, young boys played a game of football against the walls. Nearby, children skipped rope while chanting a rhyme. I passed an open doorway that led to a small courtyard and peeked inside. Clothes hung out to dry on a washing line strung between the rafters of the roof. Five doors ringed the courtyard, some wide open but no one seemed to be about. A child's bike rested against one wall. The eves of the roof sloped gently downwards until it was lower than the doorways. The tiles on the roof were green with age and looked like they were made of terracotta.

Suddenly, I heard a movement to my left and turned to see an old man sitting just inside the door. I hadn't seen him at first. I turned to leave but he beckoned me towards him. His deeply wrinkled hands rested on an old walking stick as he rocked gently back and forth. Strands of silver hair hung down from his balding head to join his long, wispy, white beard. He looked like the stereotype of the ancient Chinese philosopher. I circled the little yard with my finger and smiled, making the universal thumbs up sign of approval. He nodded and smiled in understanding. I motioned with my camera, indicating that I wanted to take his picture. His eyes lit up and he nodded his consent. When I had finished, I bowed to him slightly in thanks and left.

ৡৢঀৢ

The sun was a dull orb in the smog-filled sky as I walked across Tiananmen Square the following morning. Even the very mention of the name Tiananmen made me recall the details of the terrible events that took place there in 1989. In the weeks leading up the beginning of June that year, demonstrators had occupied the square. They protested against the Chinese government's authoritarianism and called for economic change and democratic reform. The Communist Party were not about to let this challenge to its power go unpunished. On June 4th, tanks and soldiers arrived to deliver a very clear message to those who sought change. An estimated two thousand people were killed during the brutal crushing of the demonstration. A raft of trials, executions, and long prison sentences followed for those directly or indirectly involved in the protests. As I passed by the beautiful pagoda I had seen the day before, workers were tearing it apart and throwing it into the back of a truck. I continued towards the gate of the Forbidden City.

In the days of the Emperor, death by disembowelment was the fate for anyone caught inside the Forbidden City without good reason. Nowadays, things have moved on and the hapless visitor is instead financially disembowelled by having to pay a hefty entrance fee. The days of being 'forbidden' are gone as droves of tour groups poured through the entrance gate. The vast complex of palaces and halls were home to generations of China's Emperors and is justifiably one of China's top tourist attractions.

I rented a self-guided audio tour and was happily surprised when I turned it on to hear the unmistakable voice of Roger Moore. The smooth voice of Agent 007 would be taking me through the Forbidden City.

The complex is comprised of a series of halls and courtyards that the Emperor of the day used for various duties. Each hall tried to out-do the other in terms of magnificence. I could sense a wry smile on the audio as Roger Moore introduced the 'Hall of Heavenly Purity'. It once contained twenty-seven beds where the Emperor indulged himself with the royal concubines. With barely concealed glee, Roger informed me of the bouts of bed hopping that took place there, feats that would have been worthy of James Bond himself. Apparently, one Emperor actually died from over-indulgence in that room. There are definitely far worse ways to go.

The Forbidden City was impressive but it felt like a series of empty houses with no furniture. I later learned that the Nationalist forces had taken much of the treasures with them to Taiwan in 1949 before the Communist takeover. I had a feeling that they had taken the best items with them. I left the Forbidden City and spent the rest of the day in a Starbucks coffee shop. Over cups of strong coffee, I read as much as I could about China's greatest attraction, the Great Wall.

ॐ

I joined sixteen other sleepy tourists in the hotel courtyard the following morning for a bus that would take us to the Great Wall. I felt it might be my lucky day. The smog that had plagued the city the past few days had given way to glorious sunshine. Before long, we were ushered into a minivan and started to make slow progress through Beijing's treacle-like traffic. Bicycles poured around the slow moving bus like water around a ship. Despite the ever-increasing numbers of cars on China's roads, the humble bicycle still seems to hold its own. It was hot and uncomfortable and we crushed ourselves into seats much too small for us. My knees were drawn up almost to my chest for the whole journey while a broken seat spring poked into my back. For most of the trip, I just bowed my head on the headrest in front of me and prayed hard for the journey to be over. The anticipation of seeing one of the wonders of the world eased my discomfort somewhat.

I was relieved when we finally arrived at the Great Wall, located near the small village of Jinshanling. As I approached its base, I spotted the first watchtower through the golden coloured leaves of some trees. My heart raced and my step quickened. I was about to climb the Great Wall.

On the wall, hawkers milled about selling bottles of coca-cola, postcards, and books. I briefly considered buying a towel emblazoned with the face of Mao but thought better of it. I brushed past the hawkers and walked briskly up to the highest watchtower. There, I enjoyed a fine view of the wall as it coiled like a dragon across the hilly landscape. Many famous landmarks the world over tend to be over-hyped and leave you disappointed when you finally see them. This was not one of them. From where I stood, the wall was maybe six meters wide with watchtowers every fifty meters or so. It zigzagged up steep mountain ridges and plunged into unseen valleys on the other side. My eyes traced its undulating course until only the distant dots of the watchtowers were visible on the horizon. From the watchtower, I started on the ten-kilometre walk that would follow the course of the Wall east to the small settlement at Simatai.

As I walked, a hawker joined me on my journey. She was an old woman, slightly stooped with a weathered face that made her look older than she probably was. She was dressed in a dark purple wrap tied at the waist and carried a wicker basket on her back with books and cards for sale.

"Hello, you want water, coke, very hot today," she squawked.

"No, I'm fine thanks, I already have water," I replied as I moved on quickly.

"You want card, nice book about wall?" she persisted.

"No, I'm fine thanks," I repeated as I walked on briskly.

Now, I have visited a few countries and dealt with hawkers before but this woman was the most determined one I had ever encountered. I told her repeatedly that there was no way I was going to buy a *single* card from her and that she was wasting her time with me. She asked me where I was going and I expected her to admit defeat when I told her I was heading for the distant Simatai. Instead, she kept on walking with me, up and over the crumbling ruins of the wall and down the steep embankments on the other side. At some particularly steep sections, I attacked them at a brisk pace, feeling confident that she would give up. Instead, she would scramble up ahead of me and be there at the top to offer me a bottle of water as I arrived panting and gasping for breath. It slowly dawned on me that she might even be willing to pester me all the way to Simatai. I didn't know it at the time but she had me from the very first moment. Like in the film *Jerry McGuire*, she had me at 'Hello.' She was an expert at this game and I was only a novice. I finally surrendered to her at the highest tower and I bought a pack of ten postcards and a bottle of water. Her old eyes sparkled in victory as I handed over the money. I have to say that even though I was relieved to see the old bat finally turn and take her leave of me, I couldn't help but admire her determination.

As I walked further along, the wall was in a deteriorated and crumbled state. The postcard perfection of the wall in Jinshanling gave way to broken stone and earth. Some of the watchtowers were partially collapsed. You certainly got a more authentic feeling for the wall here then you did from the sanitised version at Jinshanling. Even though the wall was very wide at the beginning, it narrowed as it went eastward and was only two meters wide in some places. I noticed that people had written graffiti on parts of the wall. Some of it was old, etched by bored soldiers of a by-gone Empire. Most of it however was new and crude.

I stopped to eat my packed lunch around the halfway point. The surrounding land looked scorched and bare. I looked out across the long stretch of stone ramparts ahead of me and tried to trace its route across China in my mind. The wall continued across grasslands, up mountains and down into valleys until finally petering out in the Gobi desert over five thousand miles away. The construction of the wall was an incredible achievement that took hundreds of years to complete. I couldn't help but wonder what was going through the minds of the Emperors who ordered it to be built? Did they really think it would keep the invaders out forever? The Chinese Emperors must have been very insecure if they felt the need to build a barrier like this. I considered that maybe it was never intended to keep out the barbarians. Maybe it was built so that they could point to it and declare, "Look how the Wall surrounds our land. We are defended. We are safe. We are secure." It is a testimony to the ineffectiveness of the wall that the invading Mongols penetrated it by merely bribing the gatekeepers. Genghis Khan is reputed to have said, "The strength of a wall depends on the courage of those who defend it." It is surely the world's greatest monument to insecurity.

I reached Simatai at the end of my trek on the Great Wall. The minivan was already waiting to take us back to Beijing. Once more, we contorted ourselves into uncomfortable positions in the cramped minibus. Even though I felt tired, it was too uncomfortable to sleep. Beijing's bright lights couldn't come fast enough.

࿔ි)࿔

Right in the middle of Tiananmen Square is Mao's final resting place. Despite his wishes to be cremated, it seemed that the central government just couldn't pass up the chance to create another tourist attraction in the city. I arrived early and joined the back of a long queue. A soldier approached me and beckoned me out of the queue. What had I done? I followed him to the front of the queue where he barked at some people to move back before placing me before them, much to my embarrassment. Being a foreigner in China does have its benefits. After a short wait, we all filed across the Mausoleum courtyard towards the building that held the former leader's body. Vendors rented bouquets of flowers for people to place inside the tomb as an offering. Cartfuls of flowers rumbled back and forth so it seemed that these flowers were reused many times a day. A short flight of steps led to a great marble statue of Mao seated on a throne. I was struck by how similar it looked to the Lincoln Memorial in Washington D.C.

I hung around the area in front of the statue for a while and watched people pay their respects. Some people bowed deeply before his giant image as if before a God. Others bowed respectfully, full of admiration. One man stood before the statue and tossed his bouquet of flowers on the ground. He fixed the statue with a withering glare that was full of hate. Despite that, there was no doubting the feeling of respect and reverence the people had for Mao. I then joined the line to see the man himself.

Just before entering the hall where he lay, the line split in two and we filed slowly around Mao's casket. His body was completely enclosed in a glass case with flowers encircling his body. A red flag with the hammer and sickle rested on his chest. A spotlight illuminated his face and made his features seemed waxen, almost fake. I couldn't shake this nagging feeling that they had buried Mao's body in the back garden years ago and replaced him with this plastic imitation in order to keep the tourists coming. Who would know the difference? A ten second glance is all you get before being ushered into the most important part of the Mausoleum, the Mao Gift Shop.

I felt a little embarrassed about even thinking of buying the

Mao towel at the Great Wall when I saw that I could get a Mao salt and peppershaker set instead. What home would be complete without one? Why stop there? Match that with the Mao tea cosy, Mao plates, Mao posters, and Mao wall-clocks. The list of items embossed with his image seemed endless. Here was the body of one of history's most devoted socialists and, within feet of his cold remains (if that's what they really are), capitalism was thriving. I don't think he would have approved.

The brisk sale in Mao memorabilia was a little hard to understand. In the West, he is generally viewed as a brutal dictator on a par with Hitler or Stalin, responsible for the deaths of millions of his people. In China, he is widely regarded as the man who brought China out of the dark ages into the modern world. When pressed about Mao and his legacy, Chinese people tend to say he was seventy percent right and thirty percent wrong. The older people still revere him even though it was they who bore the brunt of his policies. The younger people have little time for him. His Cultural Revolution and Great Leap Forward were policies that were hard to understand and caused millions to suffer.

After I left the Mausoleum, an old man approached me selling a Mao watch. The watch was cheap and had a picture of Mao on the face with his right hand acting as the second hand. I shook my head in refusal and he turned to leave. I couldn't believe it. He had given up after only one rebuff. That wasn't the spirit of the Great Wall Hawker, who harried me for five kilometres until I caved in. I shook my head in disappointment. What was hawking coming to?

The following day, I decided to embark on a little travel experiment that I had been thinking about for a while. For the modern traveller, the mystery and adventure of travel has been eliminated. With guidebooks in hand, tourists know exactly where to go, where to stay, what to visit and how to get there. I hoped to rediscover a bit of that mystery. I decided to hop on the subway at Tiananmen Square and just see where it took me. I had no aim or destination in mind at all. It was a total departure from my normal well-ordered travel routine. I felt it was time to leave the guidebook in the hotel and just see what I might find. It felt strange, not having a place to aim for but it was also exciting.

I took the subway westbound and got off at the random stop of Babaoshan. At ground level, I found myself surrounded by a forest of high-rise apartments. More were being erected in a busy and noisy construction site nearby. I passed a graveyard on my left and thought it might be worth investigating.

Leafy trees provided shade for the rows of headstones and the well-tended flowerbeds. I walked unhurriedly from headstone to headstone, trying to decipher what I could from the dates. Many of those buried there had died between 1951 and 1959. That suggested that those people died in the Korean War. I also found the graves of two foreigners, Douglas Frank Springhall and Agnes Smedley. The inscriptions on their headstones read 'Friends of the Chinese People.' I later learned that they were both devoted communists who had agitated for social change in Britain and the USA. After little success, they came to China to finish out their days.

I also learned that the graveyard had a much earlier history. In the days of the Emperor, the spot was the final resting place of the Imperial eunuchs from the Forbidden City. These castrated men made perfect recruits to the royal staff as they couldn't have children and would not be tempted to try to seize power and start a dynasty themselves. As the Emperors of

China became more and more involved with self-indulgent pleasures, many eunuchs became very powerful and wealthy. Being an imperial eunuch became a much sought after position. So much so, that many people risked the horrific operation necessary even though the chances of death were great.

At that stage, it was time to return to Tiananmen Square. I hoped to make it back in time to see the lowering of the flag ceremony, which takes place every day at sunset in Tiananmen Square. A large crowd had already assembled when I got there. I managed to muscle my way towards the front and waited for the ceremony to begin. Just as the sun started to disappear, troops emerged in formation through the Tiananmen Gate and marched across the road towards the fluttering flag of China. They were marvellous, each step perfectly synchronised. They wore green and white uniforms with their rifles resting on their shoulders. The flag was lowered with great pomp and ceremony, carefully folded, and marched back across the street into the Forbidden City for safekeeping for the night.

As the soldiers departed with their flag, the sun finally disappeared in the west and the lights in the square started to flicker on. I knew it was time to leave Beijing and continue on to the next step of my journey. Before delving deeper into China, I wanted to journey south to a city whose history has been a bloody one, the city of Nanjing.

2

THE OSCAR SCHINDLER OF CHINA

It's not usual for a German Nazi to be hailed a war hero but that is exactly what John Rabe was. Rabe was a member of the Nazi party when he arrived in China to work for Siemens in 1910. War broke out between Japan and China in 1931 and the Japanese had occupied much of the northeast of the country. Beijing and Shanghai had already fallen as the Japanese army advanced on Nanjing in November 1937. Rabe was one of the few foreigners who chose to remain behind in Nanjing and help the civilian population. After a brief siege, the city surrendered on December 13th 1937 and so began a two-month orgy of killing that has yet to be equalled.

The Nanjing Massacre Museum is dedicated to the memory of those who died in the massacre and ensures that nobody forgets the horrific events of those six weeks. Despite those that Rabe managed to save, thousands of others were not as lucky. The museum is a bloodstained account of the atrocities that occurred during that period. Large rocks lined the path to the museum and bore inscriptions describing the numerous separate massacres that made up the entire bloody event. After

Part of the city walls that once surrounded Nanjing

reading three or four inscriptions, the formula seemed to be the same. 'X number of people were killed here, machine gunned by murderous Japanese monsters. What pain!'

The museum is built around one of the mass graves that were uncovered after the war. Inside the museum, graphic charts on the walls describe the state the skeletons were found in. They make for chilling reading. One notice read 'One girl, nails in the side of her head with clear bayonet marks in her pelvic bone.' Another read 'Six year old child with skull on chest, suggesting that it had been beheaded.' Yet another read 'Sixty year old woman with bullet hole in the forehead.' People filed by each chart in a sombre mood, some covering their mouths at some particularly horrific description. The silence was broken only by the occasional sound of sobbing. Shockingly, the methods of murder were numerous. The victims were shot, stabbed, beheaded, buried and burned alive. Others were used in live bayonet and shooting practice. Hundreds of women were forced to become sex slaves in 'Comfort Stations' where they were gang raped. The list went on and on until I could read no more of it.

Faced with the excesses of the Japanese troops, John Rabe along with other foreigners established the Nanjing Safety Zone, a small area of the city where no armed forces were allowed. It was a demilitarised zone where civilians could seek refugee from the carnage. Rabe used his Nazi party membership to prevent Japanese soldiers from entering the zone. Through the efforts of Rabe and others, an estimated two hundred thousand people were saved from the bloodthirsty Japanese.

The pain that Nanjing suffered was deepened even more by the Japanese refusal to admit that their army did anything wrong during the occupation of the city. Unlike Germany, Japan has never had to apologise for its role in the war. This may have encouraged some intellectuals and academics to wonder aloud if the Japanese Army had anything to be sorry about in Nanjing. Those denials were hard to imagine in the face of the evidence that surrounded me.

John Rabe left Nanjing and returned to Germany in 1938. He wrote to Hitler about what he had witnessed but that only led to his arrest and interrogation by the Gestapo. He was forbidden to speak about what he had seen in Nanjing. After the war, he descended into poverty. He was greatly helped by regular food and money parcels sent by the grateful Chinese government. He easily deserves the name of the Oscar Schindler of China.

The Memorial finishes on an upbeat mood, talking about Sino-Japanese friendship and Japanese atonement. Even in such dark days, the ray of human compassion shone through in Nanjing in the shape of John Rabe. After a day at the museum, I felt drained and needed somewhere to re-charge the batteries. I had just the place in mind.

ஃ૭ઝ

Foot massage has a long tradition that goes back over five thousand years in China. There was a place offering foot massage near the hotel I was staying. A huge poster of a pair of feet hung above the entrance and made it hard to miss.

When I explained what I wanted, two lovely Chinese women showed me to a room with comfortable stuffed seats, hot tea, and television to watch as I waited for my massage. After a few minutes, the two women returned to the room carrying two wooden pails filled with warm dark water. I eased my tired feet out of my shoes and immersed them in the warm water. There seemed to be stones at the bottom of the pail. While my feet soaked, I received a head, neck, shoulder, and back massage that had me practically nodding off to sleep. It was just what I needed.

After my feet were dried, they were propped on a footrest, leaving me to relax for a few minutes. The women returned a little later to continue. They each kneeled at either side of me and went to work. First, they gave me a fast massage of the thighs, calves, and feet. They then rubbed cream into my feet and kneaded it hard with their knuckles. At times, they dug so deep that it bordered on pain. Throughout the massage, the two of them chatted back and forth, looking up at me and giggling. I practiced my poor Chinese with them but this only caused further fits of laughter. They then beat my feet gently with a small wooden hammer before finally running a wooden comb repeatedly over the sensitive skin. Not only did my feet glow but also my entire body felt better. The two ladies waved me off at the front door as I left the building. I headed back to the hotel as if walking on a cushion of warm air. My feet had never felt so good and neither had I.

It was Friday night and I wanted to see what Nanjing's nightlife was like. I had been told about a pub called Castlebar and, when I got there around nine, the place was already full. Chinese students and businessmen mixed with a liberal sprinkling of Westerner ex-pats. Loud Chinese rock music competed with Western hits. I met a German engineer who was working in Nanjing with Siemens. I told him about John Rabe.

"I have not heard of this person you speak of," he admitted, draining his Heineken and ordering another two bottles for us.

"The nightlife here is not that great," he said, scanning the bar.

"Not like in Shanghai. They really know how to have a good time in Shanghai," he said with a look of a man who had some good memories of the place.

The night carried on to Little Scarlet's, a nightclub used by some shady looking underworld characters. It was bright when I finally collapsed into my bed early the next morning.

I woke later that day with a throbbing head and a throat that felt like someone had stuffed it with cotton wool. I fumbled in my bag for some painkillers but could not find any. I lay on the bed, groaning with pain until I felt able to leave the room. As I got dressed, I remembered what the German engineer had told me about Shanghai. I decided to waste no time and head south for Shanghai that evening.

There is a time and place for everything and breakfast in McDonalds after a big night on the town is that time and place. The Golden Arches offered salvation for my booze-soaked system in the form of orange juice, coffee, and two breakfast sandwiches. As I ate, I noticed a young woman at the next table glancing at me. Cindy smiled and introduced herself and readily accepted my invitation to join me.

As we ate, I asked her about life in China. I didn't waste any time in getting right to the point.

"Do young people look forward to democracy in China?" I asked, my voice low for fear of anyone overhearing us.

"Young people are not concerned with that," she replied, as she slurped her Coke. I was surprised by her answer.

"But don't you want to decide what kind of government is in power?" I asked.

"Matters of government are above my understanding and are of no concern to me. Why should I, a person with no knowledge of the workings of government, decide on who should be in power? Government is for politicians and I am not a politician. I'm happy with our current system of Chinese socialism."

I was a bit amazed at this and she must have noticed the look on my face.

"I do admire your Western democracy," she admitted, taking a bite out of her chicken burger.

20

"The power to change your government at will is an amazing thing. It is also incredible to see how people are allowed to criticise the government openly. This is something I cannot understand and would not be tolerated in China."

On hearing this, I couldn't resist asking about her thoughts on the Tiananmen Square massacre.

"The killing of the students was wrong but the government had no choice. The students who protested were blinded by dreams of democracy. The government cannot allow such challenges to happen. Only the government can bring about this change."

It chilled me to hear how someone so young and educated could hold such ideas. She seemed to be only interested in making money and getting rich. I found it hard to criticise her. Her parents and grandparents probably had to endure a very tough life and now, for the first time in generations, young people had the chance to succeed and prosper. For a young person like her in China, the possibilities are infinitely better.

For the next hour, Cindy taught me some useful Chinese phrases and I wrote them into my notebook. I tried to write them as they sounded so I would be able to repeat them later. I saw her to her bus and waved her off.

გაგ

My train to Shanghai was not due to leave until later that evening so I had time to visit the old City walls. These walls used to encircle the entire town and were a whopping thirty-three kilometres long. After various wars and the Cultural Revolution, only about two thirds were left intact. I got a taxi to the base of the wall from where I hoped to get to the top. The wall was huge and traffic ran underneath it through an archway. It was also very stout and easily twice as thick as the Great Wall. I found some steps nearby and walked up the side until I was on the top.

As I wandered along the top of wall, I saw an old man flying a kite. I followed the kite line into the sky but still had trouble locating it, as it was so high. He controlled the kite with a large spool of what seemed to be wire instead of string. He seemed to be struggling with it, as if it threatened to pull him clean off his feet at any minute. Indeed, the kite was so high it could have posed a flight hazard. Chinese people of all ages seem to have a great fondness for flying kites. After admiring the wall, I descended to the street again.

Not far from the base of the wall was a Police Museum. I badly needed to visit the bathroom and went inside to use the facilities. I had a quick look at some of the displays as I tried to locate the toilets. Police museums tend to be boring and this one didn't seem any different. Who could possibly care about seeing the hat of the famous police officer Yu or the white gloves worn by detective Xi when he arrested the notorious criminal Wang? It was more like a recruitment station that anything else.

When I located the toilets, I found they were the squat type found all over Asia. Each cubicle was separated from the other by a low green partition. Only a thin trail of cigarette smoke rising from a stall betrayed an occupant. I picked a smokeless cubicle and locked the door behind me. After a few minutes, I had a strange feeling that I was being watched. I took my head up to see a man staring down at me. He had a look of surprise on his face and a cigarette dangled dangerously on the corner of his mouth. Just as I was about to say something, another head appeared over the other partition to join in staring at the foreigner. This was too much. I banged on the partition walls and shouted which scattered them as fast as they had appeared. I decided I could wait after all and left hurriedly.

I got a taxi back to the hotel and onwards to the train station. I had just started to enjoy the city and could easily have spent a few more days there. The people tended to be friendlier than in Beijing. There were not as many tourists either so that meant that I got a lot more stares. It was time to move again after my brief stay in Nanjing. Even though I had enjoyed the nightlife of Nanjing, I felt I was about to hit the real deal. As the train carried me swiftly south, I fell into a fitful sleep, dreaming of how I would soon be suckling at the teat of the Great Whore of the Orient, Shanghai.

3

SIN CITY

"What odds whether Shanghai is the Paris of the East or Paris the Shanghai of the Occident? Shanghai has its own distinctive nightlife, and what a life! Dog races and cabarets, hai-alai and cabarets, formal tea and dinner dances and cabarets, the sophisticated and cosmopolitan French Club and cabarets, the dignified and formal Country Club and cabarets, prize fights and cabarets, amateur dramatics and cabarets, theatres and cabarets, movies and cabarets, and cabarets - everywhere, in both extremities of Frenchtown (French Concession), uptown and downtown in the International Settlement, in Hongkew, and out of bounds in Chinese territory, are cabarets. Hundreds of 'em! High hats and low necks; long tails and short knickers; inebriates and slumming puritans. Wine, women, and song. Whoopee!"

This was how a guidebook gushingly described Shanghai's nightlife in 1934. By that time, Shanghai was one of the greatest ports in Asia and the centre of trade and commerce in East Asia. Shanghai was also a place where those with money could indulge in any pleasure they could imagine. Shanghai became a

Part of the Bund in Shanghai

The futuristic Pudong district of Shanghai

by-word for excess and vice. There was simply nowhere like it in the world.

I had hoped to taste a little of that legendry nightlife as I wandered along the lively street of Maoming Lu. Bright neon signs advertised an endless array of bars and discos. I started the night in a place called Judy's Too. It was very dark inside and it took a while for my eyes to adjust to the dimness. A mix of Chinese and Western customers celebrated the end of the working week. Businessmen staggered about with their ties undone, arms draped around much younger women. Heavy velvet curtains guarded private 'entertainment areas' where I imagined a racier time was had. Attractive Chinese women walked around the bar selling cigars, cigarettes, and themselves. Several other striking women sat at the bar as they scanned the room. I ordered a beer and when the barman asked for eighteen Yuan, I thought it was expensive for China but this was Shanghai after all. When I gave him the money, he looked at the notes and looked back at me as if I was deaf.

"Eighty Yuan! Eighty Yuan!" he shouted, holding up eight fingers.

I stared at him in disbelief. At that price, the beer was more expensive than in Ireland, which was saying something. I handed over the money as begrudgingly as I could. For the remainder of the evening, I was to be seen shaking my head and mouthing the words "Eighty bloody Yuan." I explored a few other places along the strip but they were all similar to Judy's Too. They were full of drunken businessmen throwing their money around and entertaining prostitutes. The nightlife was a big letdown.

I was staying in Maggie Mae's hostel in the Changing district of the city. It was outside the city centre and situated in a nice, quiet neighbourhood. The following morning, I walked around the area in search of some breakfast. I came upon a line of people queuing patiently in front of a shop selling steaming dumplings called *baozi*. I joined the line of people and watched the *baozi* being cooked. The thin pastry was filled with chopped vegetables or minced meat before being closed and immersed in a pot of boiling water. A great cloud of steam practically obscured the little shop each time the chef lifted the lid from one of those vast cauldrons.

The dumplings were fished out and placed on display at the front of the shop. They did not rest there long before being snapped up by hungry customers. They were ridiculously cheap and I bought eight of them. Combined with a cup of coffee and orange juice, it was a breakfast combination that was hard to beat and became my morning meal for the remainder of my time in Shanghai.

After breakfast, I caught the bus to one of Shanghai's biggest attractions, the Bund. In 1843, the Chinese government was forced to allow the British to set up trading stations along the banks of the Yangtze. American, French, Russian, and Japanese traders soon followed. Soon, Shanghai was home to collection of multi-national settlements. I walked along the promenade and admired the great neo-classical buildings erected by the British and Americans during the start of the twentieth century. These imposing structures were the equal of anything in London or New York. This was Shanghai's Wall Street, a place where commerce flourished and great fortunes were made. Foreign interests ran these concessions as a state within a state, completely independent of Chinese control. The foreigners had their own police force, fire brigade, and currency. At its height, there were about sixty thousand foreign residents living in the city. Yet the Bund and even Shanghai itself might not exist today were it not for the vast fortunes made in the trade of one commodity – opium.

After the British merchants established themselves in Shanghai, they imported vast amounts of opium to China in exchange for tea and silk. Foreign traders made vast fortunes from the drug trade, money that they later used to fund business ventures in banking, mining, and railways. As the drug trade increased, little heed was given to the devastating effect it had on the Chinese people. By the late nineteenth century, opium houses could be found in every town and village in the country, filled with listless addicts. By that time, opium accounted for forty-three percent of China's total imports. By 1890, an estimated ten percent of the Chinese population were opium addicts. The Chinese themselves started to cultivate the poppy until almost twenty percent of the total arable land was given over to opium production by 1930. The drug trade was having a terrible effect on the country. The way the foreign powers pushed opium on China is something that evokes bitterness in Chinese people even to this day.

If reminders of the past lined one side of the river, then the future rose dazzling from the other side. There, the soaring towers and futuristic skyline of Pudong was like something taken from a science fiction book. The impressive view is dominated by two enormous structures, the Oriental Pearl Tower and the Jin Mao Building, both over four hundred and twenty metres high. I would not have been very surprised to see small spacecraft hovering about the buildings. The Chinese government had obviously decided to rectify the insult of the foreign concessions by showing the world what a real economic power looked like.

Pudong is a symbol of China's economic might. Shanghai is already one of the busiest ports in the world and home to the fastest growing stock market. It is poised to overtake Hong Kong as the major economic city in China. The sight of a homegrown success story of Shanghai overtaking the old colonial Hong Kong would please the Chinese government greatly.

After spending the day on the Bund, I caught the bus back to the hostel. Outside the main gate, local people sat on rows of plastic tables on the footpath, eating supper from tiny restaurants. It was a warm evening and they all seemed to be having a great time. I sat at a vacant stool and looked around for a menu. The manager came over and handed me a small plastic basket. She then led me to a counter laden with various meats and vegetables, each item priced individually. She mimed putting something into the plastic basket, cooking it and eating it. This brought howls of laughter from the tables who were watching this pantomime. I understood the system and selected some meat and vegetables. I handed her my basket and enjoyed a beer while waiting for my food to be cooked. The original ingredients were returned to me as a large bowl of chunky soup. It was delicious, cheap and the perfect antidote to the expense of downtown Shanghai.

I caught the bus into town the following morning and went to Nanjing Lu, a veritable Disneyland for shopping. The street advertised every Western brand and label you can think of such as Sony, GAP, Levi's, and Wrangler. Flashing neon signs advertised a vast array of goods and services. People wandered about yapping into their mobile phones while carrying their expensive purchases in a multitude of bags on their arm. I was dizzy from all the hustle and bustle and left the street to find something better.

I found what I was looking for when I walked into the Old Quarter. It was like going through a time machine, an invisible doorway that transported me back a hundred years. The high tenement buildings of the Old Quarter made the narrow lanes seem like canyons through which flowed a crazy melting pot of honking horns, screeching bikes and wailing children. Food sizzled on grills, the smell of freshly baked biscuits wafted through the air while fish splashed frantically in pails of water. I sat down at a table and ordered a bowl of noodles. As I ate, I watched some old people playing the Chinese game of mahjong as they drank steaming cups of tea. A crowd of onlookers surrounded them, interested to see which player had the more skill and craft. Great status or *big face* as it is called in China can be obtained from a display of skill in one of these games. Of course, the crowd cannot resist telling the player what he should do and what they would have done. A murmur of approval went around after a good move was made. Conversely, a series of clucking sounds follows a poor move. A small pile of Chinese bank notes near the playing board showed that it wasn't just *big face* at stake.

The residents of the Old Quarter seemed oblivious to the wealth and excess that lay outside their narrow laneways. They seemed cocooned from it all. To me, this was a little piece of China, encircled by the Westernised mini-state of Shanghai. I was glad to have found it.

For me, Shanghai is still a state within a state. It is much more developed than most other cities in mainland China. It can boast a clean, efficient underground, light rail system, punctual buses, a thriving stock market and eighty Yuan beers. Westerners adorn many of the biggest billboards. The city is home to many foreigners who, despite living in Shanghai for years, still cannot speak a word of Chinese. In many ways, things have changed little since the days of the Bund. This wasn't the real China and it wasn't what I had come six thousand miles to see. It was time to wave goodbye to the luxuries of Shanghai and to delve deep into the heart of the dragon.

4

THE LONG RIVER

Without question, the train is the best way to travel in China. It's safe, punctual, inexpensive, and clean. Both locals and tourists alike use it. Railway lines reach across China into the remotest corners of the country, carrying goods and people across the vast state. I had committed myself to a mammoth twenty-seven hour journey that would take me from cosmopolitan Shanghai to rural Yichang and the heart of China. For the next day, that rattling, rolling metal box would be my home.

Once we left Shanghai, I walked along the train carriages to stretch my muscles. It was interesting to see the different levels of seating offered in a 'classless' Chinese train. There are four types of seat available – soft sleeper, hard sleeper, soft seat, and hard seat. Soft sleepers are the best and most expensive. They usually consist of comfortable four-berth compartments with their own washrooms, carpeted floors and fake flowers in a vase.

I had booked a berth in the hard sleeper section. Despite the name, my berth was clean and comfortable with blankets and pillows provided. Bunks are arranged in bays of six in an

The submerged gorges of the Yangtze River

open-plan type carriage. The lower bunks can be converted to seats during the day. As I passed by, most people were busy unpacking food for a lavish lunch. Some passengers dozed on the upper bunks while others struggled with luggage in the narrow walkway. Most Chinese people use the hard sleeper class when going on long journeys.

I walked through a number of other hard sleeper carriages before I reached the hard seat section at the end of the train. These were the cheapest seats available. There is no assigned seating as in other sections so it's first come, first seated. As we boarded the train in Shanghai, I saw people diving through open train windows in an attempt to secure a seat in this section. When night fell, people slept where they sat. Entire families crushed themselves into seats designed for three people. Despite this, everyone seemed to be having a good time. Adults shared homemade lunches of noodles, fried vegetables, roast chicken, and cakes while the children enjoyed sweets and soft drinks.

Back in my seat, I read my guidebook for a while. It had some fascinating details about the construction of the Three Gorges Dam, the world's greatest civil engineering project. My destination of Yichang was a short distance from the dam site. The project was the very definition of the word monumental. Once completed, the dam would stretch one and a half miles across the Yangtze and six hundred feet high, creating a reservoir upriver that would be four hundred miles long. This inland lake would enable ocean-going ships to access the heart of China and its goods. At capacity, the dam would generate the same power as sixteen nuclear power stations. Not since the Great Wall had China undertaken such a mammoth project.

The piercing voice of a woman in the next bay disrupted my reading. It sounded like a mother giving out to her children. I stuck my head around the corner to see what was going on. There, an elderly woman was wagging her finger wildly and giving out to an old man who I assumed was her husband. I had no idea what was being said to him but I could tell it wasn't good. He looked every inch the hen-pecked husband as he cowered from the stream of invective. His hands rested on his knees as he nodded in agreement with whatever she was spouting. He swayed gently back and forth as if he was in a mild trance. I'd say he wanted to be as far away from there as possible.

Not everyone on board was as unhappy as that hen-pecked husband. Leong was on his way home to Yichang for a family celebration before starting a new job in Huangzhou, outside Shanghai. He was young and fresh faced and wore a severe haircut that made me think he may have spent time in the army. He talked with pride about the construction of the Three Gorges Dam. I asked him what would happen to the people who displaced by the rising waters of the dam. He told me that many of these people would be resettled in an island outside Shanghai. New houses and schools were being built there for the settlers.

"Are the people sad to be leaving their homes?" I asked. He smiled and shook his head.

"No, no, they are happy. Now their children have a chance to make a better life, a life they never had."

I wasn't sure if Leong really believed this himself. It just sounded too convenient to me. The displacement of an estimated two million people was being promoted by the authorities as a wonderful opportunity to give the children of these peasants a start in life that their parents never had. Whatever the truth in this, it was an opportunity for which they never had a choice.

I attracted the usual interest from my Chinese neighbours. I had some interesting 'conversations' with some curious passengers through a combination of pointing at phrasebooks and hand actions. They all wanted to know the same things – "Where are you from?", "Where is your wife?", "Are you married?", "Why aren't you married?", and "How much money do you have?" It became very tiring after a while and made me very thirsty. It was time for some cheap Chinese beers from the service trolley before bed.

Leong told me that the lights were due go out at ten so I went to the small communal bathroom to wash before bed. As I brushed my teeth at the basin, a cute Chinese girl walked in and started to wash up beside me. She was sweet and innocent looking and I caught her glancing at me shyly as I washed. I was about to say something to her when she suddenly started to cough and splutter loudly. I watched in mild horror as she hocked up the yellowish contents of her lungs into the sink with a series of loud and sickening guttural sounds. She wiped her mouth with the back of her hand and smiled at me. I didn't hang around to watch her brush her teeth. At exactly ten o'clock, the train was plunged into darkness. A little while later, I drifted off into a fitful sleep as the train rattled across China.

☙ ❧

I woke the next morning to the unmistakable air of 'Flower of Scotland' playing over the speakers. Even though it was only seven in the morning, most people on the train were already awake. I couldn't get back to sleep so I ambled out to the corridor and stretched my muscles.

Outside, rural China had been awake for hours. The early morning mist was starting to lift over the trees and lakes that we passed. I sat at a small table in the corridor with a cup of tea and watched the passing countryside. We passed a field with people saving hay. There was no machinery to be seen, all the labour was manual. The men had their sleeves rolled up and were heaping the golden hay into the back of a wooden cart which was hitched to a donkey. A woman stood on top of the cart with a pike spreading each delivery around. It was very much like the way people saved hay at home in Ireland in the old days. Some time later, I saw a man pulling a wooden plough through a muddy field as another guided the yoke. This was a long way from the glitz of Shanghai.

For lunch, I cooked up another pot of spicy noodles. Noodles – I'd eaten almost nothing else since arriving in China and the thought of more made me want to scream. A constant convoy of trolleys rattled through the corridor every ten minutes selling food, drinks, magazines, and toys. I slurped my noodles to the grating sound of the woman next door berating her husband for the umpteenth time that day. Leong translated a public announcement and informed me that the train's arrival in Yichang would be delayed by two hours. The Chinese seemed to take this news in their stride as I cursed and settled in for a few more boring hours on the train. Even though it was nice to talk with the locals, it was a strain, as their English was poor and my Chinese non-existent. It required a huge amount of concentration to understand what they were trying to say. I felt weary after a few hours of this and, feigning a headache, retreated to my bunk to rest.

Before arriving in Yichang, I asked Leong if he had any recommendations on where to stay. He gave me the names of a few hotels and phoned his father to get some more suggestions. Of course, I was really angling for an invite to his home and to the party. After all, isn't that what the legendary Chinese hospitably is all about, taking in the hungry traveller, feeding him and giving him somewhere to lay his head? I had imagined being welcomed into Leong's home like a long lost son. A large glass of rice wine would be thrust into my hand before I'd be shown to a table creaking with foods of indescribable deliciousness. After we had eaten to bursting point, we would all sing and dance the night away. When the night was finished, I'd be shown to a soft and comfortable bed where the beautiful and busty daughter of the house would come to visit me after everyone else had gone to sleep for some serious romantic misunderstanding.

The shuddering train snapped me out of my daydream. We had arrived at Yichang. I said my goodbyes to Leong and wished him all the best in his future job. As I left the carriage, I stopped next to the hen-pecked husband.

"You should really finish her off with the back of a shovel when you get home," I advised him, jerking my thumb at his wife.

Even though he didn't speak a word of English, I swear he smiled back at me with a knowing smile. Maybe he had just that very plan in mind.

I got a taxi to one of the hotels Leong had recommended. The taxi driver who brought me there followed me into the lobby and the only English he seemed to know was "Where you go tomorrow?" and "What time will I collect you?" He seemed to be under the impression that he would be my taxi driver for my time in Yichang. Bless him.

After I freshened up, I walked the short distance to the ferry terminal to book my ticket for the Yangtze River ferry the following day. Poor looking stalls lined the road along the river along with an unusual number of hairdressers. The city had a deprived and dangerous edge to it and I felt nervous walking along the darkened streets. I guessed that many of the people displaced by the rising river had ended up here instead of the island paradise that Leong had mentioned. I was sure that those refugees would provide the city with poor and destitute for years to come.

The ferry hall was deserted when I arrived but I still

managed to find a friendly girl with some English to help me purchase my ticket. I wanted to get a boat upriver to the city of Chongqing, a mammoth journey of over five hundred kilometres. I had two options to get there – I could take the fast thirteen-hour hydrofoil, or take the three-day river cruise. I didn't fancy a long river journey so I bought the hydrofoil ticket. I emphasised to the girl that I wanted to pass through the Three Gorges Dam and she nodded her head in understanding and confirmed that the hydrofoil would indeed go through the dam site. Satisfied, I paid for my ticket and left.

On the way back to the hotel, I popped into a busy looking restaurant for supper. The menu was in Chinese so I had to resort to the old point-and-order technique. This consisted of wandering slowly along the various tables and staring at what people were eating. When I saw a dish that looked good, I would stop at the table, causing the occupants to cease their eating and conversation suddenly while I called a waiter over. This time, I chose poorly as a plate of fatty bacon with ginger and vegetables arrived at my table. A bowl of onion soup, rice, and a bottle of beer helped save it from being a complete disaster.

As I tried to pick some food from my meal, I watched a stout young child running amok around the restaurant. His parents were smiling and laughing as the tubby little devil roamed the restaurant, tormenting people at will. He was clearly disturbing people trying to enjoy their meal but his parents didn't seem to care. He was obviously a child that was given everything he demanded, a little Emperor. I guessed he was one of the millions of other little Emperors that China's one-child policy had spawned over the last few decades. He finally saw me and rumbled over to me, folds of fat giggling under his t-shirt. He started kicking my leg and laughing, his face bulging and red from the effort. Normally, Chinese people would be very shy of Westerners but not this one. How I wished I could pick him up by the legs and dunk his head repeatedly into my cold soup. I even had to suffer the indignity of rushing my last drop of beer just to get away from the little bastard. As I left, I turned to see the father laughing hard, pieces of food dropping from his mouth as his spawn ate the fatty bacon I had left on my plate.

ॐꝏ

I wandered down to the ferry hall with my bags early the following morning, still yawning and rubbing the sleep from my eyes. Even at that early hour, the streets were buzzing with activity. People were cycling to work and doing their morning exercises. I saw one man running backwards and I remembered reading somewhere that people believed doing this was supposed to reverse ageing and make you younger. Along the road, stalls dispensed hot and cold food to people going on boat trips. I got an orange-like drink and dry bread for my breakfast. Despite the food, I was excited. Seeing the Three Gorges Dam was to be one of the highlights of my trip.

I was directed to a bus after showing my ferry ticket, which I was told would take me to the hydrofoil. The bus left Yichang and continued out of the city. I could see the Yangtze River and felt we should be on the boat at that stage if we were going to pass through the dam. The dam site was about an hour's bus journey outside Yichang. My growing fears were confirmed an hour later when we passed under a concrete archway announcing our arrival at the Three Gorges Dam project site. I realised then that the bus was going to drop us beyond the dam from where we would get the hydrofoil. I was gutted. We were deposited at a gleaming ferry hall. Through the mist, I caught a glimpse the great dam, a behemoth of construction just visible in the distance. I couldn't even get a decent photograph of it. I thought about going back to Yichang and trying to visit the dam the following day but I decided to accept my fate and press on.

The journey on the hydrofoil failed to lift me out of my depression. My seat must have been the worst on the entire boat, offering me a great view of the engines and little else. It was a foggy, misty day and was set to continue like that. However, the journey on the river was smooth and fast, even if the scenery wasn't great. I pulled out my guidebook and read an interesting but terrifying section about what can happen when dams go bad.

One of the main advantages touted of the Three Gorges Dam will be flood control. The designers claim that the dam will be able to tame the Yangtze River and make such catastrophic floods that have drowned millions of people a thing of the past. Dams had already been used to control flooding for decades in China. Sometimes, the very dams that were designed to control floods can themselves lead to disaster as happened in 1975.

The Yellow River is China's second longest river and has flooded numerous times in the past with terrible loss of life. Flooding in 1887 drowned over one million people, 1931 over two million, and in 1938 seven hundred thousand. The Banqiao Dam had been built in an attempt to try to control the murderous flooding of the Yellow river. The dam was designed to withstand a 'once in a thousand years' flood. However, a typhoon in August 1975 produced rainfall in one day that exceeded the annual levels. The dam wasn't able to cope with the weight of water and burst. This created a tsunami-like wave ten kilometres wide that swept all before it. The force of water set off a domino effect that breeched another sixty dams along the river.

For years, details about the disaster had been declared a state secret and the death toll was unknown. The details were declassified in 1995 and reports showed that over two hundred thousand people had drowned or died of disease due to the

Banqiao dam break. It was chilling to think what would happen if something similar were to befall the Three Gorges Dam.

All along the river's steep banks, new high-rise buildings clung like barnacles to rocks. These were the new towns being built for people displaced by the dam. The dam had already raised the water level by ten metres so many villages were already under water. It was not only human settlements that were being submerged by the rising waters. The Three Gorges were a stretch of narrow canyons that were traditionally the most beautiful but dangerous section of the river. It took great skill to navigate through the churning waters that powered through the gorges. As I feared, they had also disappeared beneath the rising waters of progress. What was once one of China's most dangerous river trips had been reduced to nothing more that a boring river commute.

On the hydrofoil, the passengers were kept entertained by a series of Kung Fu films starring Jackie Chan. I ordered lunch and got a meal of rice, vegetables, and a bonus mystery meat. I prodded the meat with my chopsticks, trying to discern what animal it came from but I soon surrendered to hunger and quickly wolfed the meal down. As I ate, my neighbour stared at me without pause. He was an elderly man who worn an old-fashioned blue tunic from the Mao era. During the entire meal, he stared at me with his eyes bulging and mouth agape, barely breathing. Once I finished, I left my seat just to get away from his unsettling stare.

I stepped outside on the small deck of the hydrofoil to get some air. The boat was going at great speed and the wind and spray tore at my jacket. I studied the face of the cliffs for any signs of the mythical Ba people. The Ba were a mysterious tribe that occupied the area before the arrival of the Chinese. They were remarkable mainly for the way they buried their dead. They would scale the cliffs with the dead in a cedar coffin and leave it hanging there. Some were left in caves high up on the cliff face while other dangled by a rope at the end of a wooden platform. Nobody is sure how they did this or why.

Ships big and small plied the great river. The Chinese call the Yangtze River *Chang Jiang* – The Long River. Giant freighters laden with coal ploughed towards Chongqing, as did barges carrying trucks and cars. We sped by tourist ships as they ambled slowly along the river with their very bored looking passengers. On the far shore, people fished using long bamboo poles with nets attached to the ends. I watched a fisherman hauling his meagre looking catch onto a long boat with a semi-cylindrical roof. He looked up as we whizzed by. For a split second, I caught his gaze and we regarded each other with mutual curiosity. I wondered what he thought, seeing a Westerner standing on a boat as it sped towards Chongqing while he tried to scratch out a living from the river. I raised my hand in salute and, as he faded quickly into the distance, I could see him slowly raise his hand and wave back at me.

ༀ

For years, Chongqing was a sleepy city, only famous for being one of the four "furnaces" of China. Temperatures there during the summer months would regularly exceed forty degrees Celsius (a hundred and four degrees Fahrenheit). The city's days in the shade are coming to an abrupt end thanks to the Three Gorges Dam. Ocean going ships will be able to sail up the Yangtze to Chongqing and open it up to the world. The Chinese government are well aware of this and created a new municipality around the hinterland of the city in 1997 under its direct control. The population of this new municipality is an estimated thirty five million, making it the biggest city in China.

After arriving in the city, I found a hotel with dorm rooms not far from the main plaza. The hotel looked worn but was cheap and central. The communal bathroom was a small tiled affair with a squat toilet and a rubber nozzle sticking out of the wall, pretending to be a showerhead. Man's dream of being able to have a shit and a shower at the same time was a reality.

I left the hotel and walked towards the main plaza. A light but steady drizzle had been falling since I arrived. I moved slowly through a sea of multi-coloured umbrellas. The Liberation Monument was the main focal point of the plaza and other streets radiated out from it like spokes on a bicycle wheel. The monument commemorated the end of the bloody war with Japan in 1945. A young performer clad in a white suit strutted and gyrated around a stage at the base of the monument while bellowing Chinese songs to the passing shoppers. Nobody stopped to listen.

Beyond the plaza, I found some street vendors selling food. People were able to eat their food at plastic tables and chairs arranged just off the street. I wandered along the vendors, looking for something familiar. The food was buffet style where you could select what you liked and have it cooked for you. I surveyed the baskets of obscure meats with trepidation. It's one thing to be adventurous with food but another to be in the dark as to what you're being adventurous with. I tried to avoid any surprises and just went for vegetables. Even this turned out to be trickier than I expected. I handed my selection to the cook and sat at a table to wait for it to be fried. When it arrived, I discovered what I took to be small chopped tomatoes to be in fact a pig's tail.

Once again, I ate alone in a new city. I watched other tables enviously as groups of friends laughed and shared a joke, feeling happy at being able to share an occasion together. I chewed on my grisly meal and sighed. There were times during the trip when it would have been great to have someone to share the highs and lows with. However, as a solo traveller, I could choose to visit what I wanted, when I wanted. This freedom to determine my own trail was important to me.

"Where are you from?" The well-worn question came from the table behind me. I turned to face a man about thirty years old with long black hair and a thin face. He was well dressed in a shiny Chinese-style jacket. He spoke excellent English with a slight American accent. He introduced himself as William, using his English name. It was common practice among educated Chinese people to have an English name as well as their Chinese one. We spoke for a while and he explained he was in fact one of Chongqing's city planners.

"I have something to show you," he smiled as he dipped his hand into his jacket and produced a few long and polished pieces of wood.

"Please, you must look, this is my hobby," he said, offering me one of the pieces. I took one and examined it. They were watches, highly ornamental ones. They were crafted from flat pieces of black wood and were in odd and drooping shapes, like the clocks in that famous painting by Salvador Dali. The numbers on the watch face seemed to be in a random order so telling the time was difficult. I noticed the hands weren't moving and shook the watch.

"Oh no, the watches do not work," William explained.

"They don't work?" I repeated, disbelieving.

"The function is not at all important, it is the beauty of the thing that is important," he said, throwing his hair back with a bit too much drama. I handed the watch back with a smile, wondering if the people of Chongqing knew their city was in the hands of this man.

As we spoke, a young man carrying a long wooden pole on his shoulders stopped to talk to William. They seemed to know each other. He wore a shabby woollen sweater and baggy trousers, bound around his waist with some blue cord. He was also missing his two front teeth. William explained that the young man was one of the thousands of itinerant labourers that work in Chongqing called bang-bang men.

"They come from the surrounding areas, from poor villages. They come to the city to find work and send money back to their families."

I asked William what the pole was for.

"The wooden pole is called the bang-bang and it is how they get the name."

He shouted something to the young man and he placed the pole across his shoulders in demonstration.

"This is how they carry heavy items across the city," William explained. "He has a rope to attach the item to both ends of the pole. I have used him before to carry a fridge from the river to my home. He is a very good bang-bang man, very strong."

William again fired some rapid questions to the bang-bang man who seemed to drop his head as if ashamed.

"I asked him how much money he made today but he does not tell me," William said.

"I think he did not have a good day today so maybe he made around ten Yuan (one Euro)," he said, drinking his coffee.

I felt sorry for the bang-bang man. His was a tough and brutal life on the streets of the city. He was at the mercy of the whims of others, there to fill the role of a pack animal, to carry heavy goods for very little reward. He represented an army of thousands who find themselves in that role in the steep and cruel streets of Chongqing.

The river had affected the lives of all those I had encountered along its path. The rising waters promised hope and prosperity to some, poverty and desperation for others. China is one of the few nations on earth that has the power to dam such a river and displace millions of its people without their permission. The face of central China will be changed forever because of this.

47

Despite the dam, the mighty Yangtze continues to flow, bringing both sorrow and joy as it has been doing for centuries.

5

SNAKE BLOOD AND TEA

The ear cleaner was busy practicing his dark art as I tried to enjoy my tea. His victim sat on a wicker chair, his head tilted slightly to enable the ear cleaner better access. I could hear the metallic sound of the tweezers probing in his inner ear canal for something to remove. The victim's eyes were closed and his hands were folded on his knee. He looked serene, almost as if he were asleep. That was until he winced when the tweezers probed too deeply. With great fanfare, the cleaner produced a small blackish object from the man's ear and made a big fuss of displaying it to everyone. I watched all this with mild horror. The victim seemed relieved, a mixture I am sure of having the black matter removed from his ear and having the procedure over. Once he had finished, the ear cleaner put his tools away and started towards me. I was already waving my hand in refusal even before he approached my table. I hadn't bargained for minor brain surgery at a Chengdu teahouse.

I had come upon the teahouse completely by chance. After arriving in Chengdu by bus, I booked into a hostel called Sam's Guesthouse near the main square and started to explore the

Enjoying some local company in a hot-pot restaurant

Playing Chinese Dominoes in the People's Park

city. I spotted an interesting looking street off the main thoroughfare and went to investigate it. Suddenly, I found myself in a narrow avenue lined with old Chinese tea houses. The noise and traffic of modern Chengdu disappeared as I walked along the leafy laneway. I decided to have some tea and selected a teahouse with some lovely old wicker chairs. Trees that grew outside supported the roof of the building and the clay tiles on the roof were green with age. I ordered some tea and it soon arrived, served in a decorated porcelain cup with strainer and lid. After serving the tea, the waiter took it on himself to show me how to drink Chinese tea properly. First, he placed some tealeaves in the cup before adding boiling water from an old and battered looking copper kettle. He then placed the porcelain lid on the cup, allowing it to brew for about three minutes. He returned to throw the tea water onto the street and topped up the tealeaves with more boiling water. When the cup was nearly full, he lifted the kettle high so that the boiling water tumbled into the cup from a height. This was meant to agitate the tealeaves and improve the flavour. He motioned an invisible cup to his lips, indicating that it was ready to drink. I settled back into my wicker chair and sipped the refreshing tea. It was a very relaxing way to spend a day.

Teahouses have been the traditional meeting places in China. People would come not only to drink tea but also to meet friends, relax, and chat. Numerous business deals were struck over steaming cups of jasmine tea while others debated politics. It was for that reason that teahouses were closed down by the Communists during the Cultural Revolution. Such restrictions have eased in recent years and teahouses are making a comeback.

As I finished my tea, I watched some young men playing a game of mah-jong in the teahouse across the street. A businessman seated next to me shouted into his mobile phone while others ignored him and watched life go by. Shoeshine boys followed the ear cleaners and eyebrow pluckers as they wandered up and down the lane looking for business. Life seemed to move a slower pace with a cup of hot tea in your hands. Feeling suitably refreshed, I took my leave of that charming teahouse. When I tried to pay, the owner stoutly refused my money. I left feeling glad that I had discovered such a place.

ༀཅ༇

Chengdu is the capital of the populous province of Sichuan and a major hub in south-west China. I had visited Chengdu previously in 2002 and was eager to sample some of the things that I had enjoyed then. One of these was hot-pot, the speciality meal of Sichuan. I'd been told that there were some good hot-pot restaurants not far from where I was staying. Later that evening, I left Sam's to find these restaurants. The first place I investigated was empty and forlorn looking but the second one was heaving with smiling and happy looking diners. It was an easy choice. A table was found for me and cleaned by wiping the leftovers onto the floor. The table had a big hole in the middle where the waiter placed a large metal bowl of broth. He then lit a gas flame underneath the bowl and before long, the broth was bubbling. The pot was divided in two parts, one section filled with a mild chicken broth while the other contained a fiery brew, reddened with hot local chillies. This is supposed to symbolise the Yin and Yang, the mild and the fiery, the female and the male traits of life.

As is the case in other cities in China, I had a selection of meat and vegetables to choose from. In that restaurant however, all the food was on wooden skewers. The meat skewers were thicker than the vegetable ones so that once the meal was finished, the used skewers were then counted and your bill calculated. I also got a beer to help wash down the dinner and to cool my mouth from the hot spices. I placed my selection of skewered meat and vegetables upright in the boiling pot and waited for them to cook. Once I was satisfied they were well done, it was time to try some food from the spicy pot. The meat tasted fine at first but soon a surge of heat rose from my stomach and had me gasping for a mouthful of beer. It would be a few minutes before I was ready to try some more. I was enjoying the experience as sweat poured down my face.

The people of Chengdu have a reputation for being fun-loving and enjoying life. Around me, people celebrated birthdays and enjoyed family meals together. The table next to mine took a great interest in my cooking techniques and watched carefully as I shuffled food into my mouth with chopsticks. I raised my glass of beer to them in a toast. One of the men from the table stood up gingerly and staggered over to me. Without a word, he placed two glasses on the table and filled them from a bottle of baijiu (rice wine, the firewater of China). He raised his glass, pointed at the other glass and then to me. I sensed that other tables around me had stopped eating to watch this minor drama unfold. Nothing short of national pride was at stake and I wasn't about to let my country down. With a shout of *gan bei* (dry the cup), we crashed our glasses together and drank the fiery liquid in one go. A cheer rose from the other table and I was invited to join them.

Their group consisted of Bijou Man's brother, sister, and her three kids. I spent an enjoyable evening in their company. Despite their lack of English and my lack of Chinese, we managed to communicate. His brother was an engineer and a very friendly person. He taught me some local Chinese slang while Bijou Man continued to challenge me to drink. Between us, we managed to finish the whole bottle by the end of the evening. When I left, Bijou Man had to be steadied by his brother as I waved goodbye to them and staggered back to the hostel.

I woke the next morning with a terrible hangover. I somehow managed to peel myself from the bed and into a shower. After some food, I felt I could just about face into the day. I left the guesthouse and walked the short distance to the main square. I took a few photographs of the colossal statue of Mao, one of the few surviving statues of that size in China. During his reign, such statues adorned every town square in the country but after his death, most of them were torn down. He was in his traditional pose, arm outstretched across the square as if saluting a vast crowd. A pigeon rested on his hand, looking both perplexed and proud that so many people had turned out to photograph it. Another perched on Mao's head, adding to the already lavish smattering of droppings. Around the square itself, cranes and bulldozers worked ceaselessly as the city built a new underground.

Before the bulldozers reached them, I wanted to see what remained of Chengdu's old town. The old town was full of narrow streets and old buildings. Small low wicker chairs stood outside decorative archways that led to small courtyards. Large heavy wooden doors, blackened with age, guarded the entrance to ancient homes. Richly carved wooden roofs jutted out above some of the doorways. However, these historic homes were due to be torn down in order to make way for new housing developments. Many people along the street had accepted their fate and abandoned their homes. Some of the old buildings had Chinese characters daubed on the walls. As I stared at messages blankly, a young man sidled up beside me.

"Hello. Can you read the Chinese?" he inquired. I admitted that I couldn't.

"Allow me to translate. It says that the people here are protesting at being forced out of their homes, the homes of their ancestors. They don't want to go and they ask the government to allow them to stay."

With that, he nodded and left me as suddenly as he had appeared.

ॐ

After leaving the old town, I went in search of a market that I had visited during my last trip to Chengdu. I eventually found it and wandered about excitedly, hoping to see some bizarre produce for sale. I was to be disappointed as I saw nothing more exotic than ducks and pigs. It wasn't like the last time I was there in 2002.

That was my first time in China and I was tracing a route across the south west of the country from Hong Kong to Chengdu and back down to Vietnam. I had befriended Tom, Paul, and Matt while staying in a Chengdu hostel and one day, we decided to explore one of the markets in the city. Along with the usual market fare, there were some more remarkable items for sale. Skinned dogs hung from their feet in one stall and pig's heads were impaled on spikes at another. Tom took plenty photographs of the exotic fare and was endlessly writing notes into a small notepad that he kept. He told us he was writing a blog about his travels in China and that it had become very popular. Paul was a sensitive type and seemed to be slightly repulsed by what he saw.

However, it was the snakes that held us spellbound. Baskets of live snakes were for sale and we were mesmerised by the sight of those coiling, hissing reptiles. Matt, a streetwise American with good Chinese, asked the vendor to take one of the snakes out of the basket so we could photograph it. The vendor selected a five-foot snake with yellow and black markings and held it up for us. Camera flashes went off in unison as we all took our shots. There was a brief discussion between the vendor and Matt. He turned to us smiling.

"This guy wants to know how much will we offer for the snake?" he said, trying to stifle a smile.

We all laughed. We only wanted a photograph of the snake, not to buy it. The vendor produced a calculator and punched in his price, showing it to us. There was a murmur of excitement and we looked at each other.

"Hey, it'll only cost us about two bucks each and we can own our very own snake. How cool is that?" cried Tom, barely containing his excitement as he scribbled frantically into his notebook.

We handed over a wad of bank notes to the snake vendor, who deposited our purchase into a mesh bag, tied at the top with a drawstring. That was how a giddy group of travellers became the owners of a five-foot long snake.

We all took turns peering in at our purchase and laughing in disbelief. We hailed a taxi but the driver refused to take us when he saw our extra 'passenger'. Foreigners attract a lot of attention in China but with a snake, it's practically front-page news. Cyclists would pass us and do a double take at the snake in the bag, nearly crashing in the process. We were turned away from a few restaurants when they saw the snake with us. We got back to the guesthouse and managed to sneak our new guest into the dorm. Now that we'd bought a snake, what were we going to do with it? Paul was in favour of making a bold statement for wildlife and wanted to release it. Tom was in favour of keeping it and writing a book about his travels around China with his pet snake. Matt, being the hungriest, wanted to eat it.

Matt won out so we agreed to eat the snake. We met some of the kitchen staff and they agreed to cook and prepare it but we would have to kill it. One of them instructed us how to do it. I held the snake tight as Matt used his penknife to bleed the snake into a bowl. Once it was dead, the staff took over. One man slid a knife down the length of the snake and peeled his skin back expertly. The flesh was sliced up and cooked in a spicy stew. He took four small cups and poured the snake blood into them, mixing the blood with some rice wine. He then ordered us to drink. We weren't too sure about it but nobody protested so we toasted to our continued good health and downed the snake blood. It was soon followed by snake stew served with rice. The snake tasted a lot like fleshy fish and I don't think I'll be looking for more.

I snapped out of my reminiscing and wandered back to the guesthouse. On the way, I stopped into The People's Park, a big rambling area of greenery in the heart of the city. It was a lovely warm day and I wandered around happily, investigating things. A leafy replica of the Great Wall ran along one side of the park, similar to the one I had seen in Tiananmen Square. Not far from this, stood a tall obelisk monument dedicated to the communists who died fighting for Chinese freedom. In another part of the park, tables of people pitted their wits against each other in games of mah-jong and dominoes. The clack-clack sound of domino pieces being shuffled by thirty tables of elderly people filled the air. People fished in the small lake at the middle of the park while couples kissed in the shaded privacy of some bushes. I walked around the small lake to the other side. There, I found an area where old people were singing karaoke. When they saw me, they tried to get me to sing with them but I refused and spared them the ordeal.

There was plenty of hot and cold food available from stalls near the lake. I looked over a few different dishes before going for a bowl of noodles with meat and vegetables. While I tucked into my dish, another Westerner joined me at my table. Joe was from South Africa and we soon discovered that we would be on the same train bound for Xian that evening. After we finished our meal, we agreed to look for each other on the train.

I left the park and walked along the streets of Chengdu as evening closed in. Lights started to flicker on in the homes and shops along my route. I walked along the friendly streets and enjoyed the feeling of the warm air of evening. I felt I had found one of China's most relaxed and enjoyable cities. From its charming teahouses to its rambling parks, I could easily have spent another few weeks in its welcoming embrace. It was the most liveable city I had visited in my trip so far.

6

THE BROKEN ARMY

In March 1974, three peasants were digging a well outside the city of Xian when they broke through to a buried chamber. Once the dust had cleared, they peered into the vault and were struck dumb by what they saw. The floor of the underground chamber was strewn with broken pieces of clay heads, legs, and arms. The peasants hauled out some of the first pieces of the Terracotta Army to have seen the light of day in nearly two thousand years. It would turn out to be an archaeological discovery on a par with that of King Tutankhamen's tomb in Egypt. What those simple peasants discovered that day would change Xian forever and put it firmly on the tourist map. The Terracotta Army was the only reason I was going to Xian.

I managed to find Joe on the train to Xian that evening. He introduced me to Rosie, his travelling partner from Australia. I sat on a spare bunk in their berth and we shared a few bottles of beer from the service trolley and spent an enjoyable evening swapping travel stories. Rosie had been working as a commodities trader in London before taking a career break while Joe was seeing the world after finishing University. Joe and Rosie told

The ranks of the Terracotta Army

Muslim men at the Grand Mosque, Xian

me they had met in Beijing and had been travelling together since. Rosie was a bubbly character and seemed to be the perfect travel partner for the more reserved Joe.

After we arrived in Xian, we all booked into the comfortable Shu Yuan Hostel in the centre of town. Rosie and Joe left soon after to explore the area while I stayed in the room to catch up on some reading. The visit to Xian was to be another of those big moments in my trip. The previous Christmas, I had bought my father a medium-sized globe. However, I was the one who was always consulting it when I was planning my trip. When my finger drifted along my proposed route through China, it would always pause at Xian. I'd jab the spot repeatedly with my finger and mutter, "Yeah, that should be an interesting place."

I wanted to read up a little on the Terracotta Army before my visit to the site the following day. I remembered that I had seen a small travel desk just inside the main entrance to the hostel so I went there to pick up a few leaflets. An old man sat on a wicker chair next to the desk, smoking his pipe. I greeted him and he replied in English. He inquired if I had visited the Terracotta Army yet. I replied that I had not but was going there the following day.

"I will tell you some history of these warriors," he said, shifting slightly in his chair.

"They were built for China's first emperor, the great Qin Shihuang. He was a very interesting man," he said, puffing on his pipe. After a long pause, I prompted him to tell me more and he seemed happy to oblige.

"Qin Shihuang conquered many of the states that existed in China around 220 B.C. and thus unified the country for the first time. He started the Great Wall of China and built many roads, dams, and canals throughout the land. He also standardised the units of currency, weights, and measures across China. He introduced a system of local government that persists in many parts of the country to this day. However, most important of all, he created one script for all Chinese people. Without that, there would be no China. Yes, he was a very great man."

He relaxed into his chair and puffed his pipe again with a happy and satisfied look on his face. He was obviously very proud of his ancient forebear. I had read that China's first Emperor had achieved all these goals by brutal means and I pressed him on that point.

He took the pipe from his mouth and nodded.

"It is true," he conceded, "that he was brutal. He seems to have cared little for the lives of the simple peasant people and many thousands of them died in his grand construction projects." He held his pipe away from his face as if frozen in time. His face seemed full of thought and contemplation.

"A great man," he muttered as he slid his pipe inside his breast pocket and ambled away.

ༀ ཨོཾ ༀ

The following morning, we caught a local bus from Xian to the site of the Terracotta Army, about twenty kilometres outside the city. Rosie wore her blue down-lined jacket, which she was rarely separated from. When I teased her about it, she boasted that the jacket had saved her on many cold nights during her time in China and that she wouldn't be parting with it easily.

On the road to the warriors, we passed a wooded hill, which is all that remains of what was once the magnificent mausoleum pyramid of Emperor Qin Shihuang. It was hard to imagine but according to ancient historians, it was one of the grandest burial complexes ever constructed. Seven hundred thousand conscripted workers and slaves toiled on its construction for eleven long years. The two hundred and fifty foot high pyramid stood over an underground complex measuring four square miles that contained palaces, protective walls, and even a cemetery. Inside the complex, the Emperor's body lay in the middle of a scale model of the empire he had conquered. The dome of the complex was said to be studded with precious stones to represent the sky while streams of mercury represented the rivers of China. All that grandeur has now disappeared and all that is left is a small hill. He protected his final resting place with a mighty army of clay warriors that would withstand time better than his necropolis did.

Once we arrived at the site, we followed signs to the main entrance. The route led us through a gaggle of souvenir vendors. They were determined to slow our progress by taking turns to offer us terracotta warrior souvenirs. As soon as one vendor had been rebuffed, another would jump in front of us to take his place. It was like a medusa head of hawkers. It took a further ten minutes before we reached the ticket booth and the main entrance.

The site of the warriors was impressive. It consisted of a large plaza with a Circle Vision centre, an information centre, the excavation pits, and an exhibition hall. We first visited the exhibition hall, with its beautiful restored chariot and rider and other magnificent treasures. We then visited the Circle Vision building where we watched an audiovisual documentary about the background history of the Terracotta Army. The show was very bloody and gory in parts.

We then visited Pit Two where excavation work was still in progress. I peered into the pit and saw the broken state that the warriors were first found in. A peasant revolt after the death of the oppressive emperor Qin Shihuang led to the plundering of his grand mausoleum and Terracotta Army. As I leaned over the railing to get a better look into the pit, I could see that the warriors had taken an awful battering. Headless statues were half-buried in the earth. Arms, hands, and legs lay strewn around the ground. Broken chests and heads emerged from the clay, in the hope of reassembly one day.

We then walked to Pit Three, which is smaller but more impressive than Pit Two, with a few fully restored soldiers in battle array. Here, some of the warriors had been restored but most were without their heads for some reason. All of them had an arm extended, holding nothing but air where once they had held a weapon. Originally, the warriors had been armed with an impressive array of real weapons such as swords, spears, and crossbows. After being excavated, some of the bronze weapons were still sharp, which is a great compliment to the metallurgists of the time. Despite the thousands of artefacts already unearthed in the area, archaeologists believe that the Terracotta Army is only the tip of the iceberg. Xian will be yielding treasures for China for decades to come.

Every postcard scene of the Terracotta Army comes from Pit One. This massive excavation is enclosed in a hangar-like warehouse. A walking track encircles the pit so that tourists can peer down at the assembled warriors. Rosie and Joe snapped photographs of the warriors from the elevated platform as I marvelled at military ranks below me. Over a thousand clay warriors are marshalled into a well-organized battle array composed of infantry and cavalry. They stare blankly ahead, forever looking forward to the day of battle that will never come.

It is said that no two faces of the warriors are the same. Some historians suggest that each statue's face was modelled on an actual living person. Whatever the truth, many of the warriors I saw had different expressions. The narrow eyes and wry smile of one soldier seemed to communicate confidence and experience in battle. Another face was big and round and seemed to be trusting, honest, and simple. I got the feeling that it was almost as if a real army had been instantly turned to clay by some evil wizard, forever capturing their expressions at that point in time over two thousand years ago.

After we left the pits, Joe went to the gift shop to pick up a few postcards. He returned to where Rosie and I were waiting in an excited state.

"You'll never guess who I saw signing autographs in the gift shop," he cried as he beckoned us to follow him. We entered the gift shop and walked over to where a crowd had gathered around an old man signing postcards and books.

"This is one of the peasants who discovered the Terracotta Army," Joe whispered. The old man was seated behind a desk, puffing on a large cigar and posing for photographs with tourists. His forehead was heavily creased and his eyes were watery and sad looking. Once the significance of his find was realised, he was moved off his plot of land and onto a similar holding outside the city. While others got rich from the discovery, he got very little reward.

After a long day at the site, we were ready to return to Xian. We left the complex and once more battled our way past the souvenir vendors. This was where they were at their most determined and you could hardly hear yourself above the shouts of, "warriors here, cheap price, good quality, lookie, lookie."

On the way to the bus, a young girl ran up to me holding a foot high replica of a warrior.

"You like warrior, you take now, only ten Yuan for you," she rattled off repeatedly. She was dressed in ragged clothes and had no shoes. I felt sorry for her so I bought the warrior statue from her. As soon as she had the money, she ran off as fast as she had appeared. I climbed on board the bus and proudly displayed my purchase to Joe and Rosie.

"Ah, that's so cute," said Rosie, taking it from me. As soon as she did, the arm fell off the statue.

"Not to worry, some glue will fix that," Joe said, trying to stifle a smile. The head and other arm had fallen off the statue before we had reached Xian. At least we all had a good laugh at the thought of the little girl telling her friends what she had sold to a tourist.

ॐ

Xian is home to a sizeable population of Muslims who originally came from central Asia. Despite being integrated with the Chinese people, they still retain their distinctive dress and customs. Chinese Muslims are called Hui and are easily identified by the white caps and scarves worn by the men and women. The Grand Mosque of Xian was noted in my guidebook as being one of the oldest mosques in China so I made my way to the Muslim Quarter to see it.

Once I got there, the mosque wasn't exactly what I had expected. The building had neither the distinctive onion-shaped dome nor traditional minaret that people usually associate with a mosque. Except for some Arabic lettering and decorations, it would be hard to distinguish it from a Chinese temple. It had been in existence for over one thousand years and was an interesting place to wander around. An incessant conveyer belt of Western and Chinese tourists streamed through the building, all led by flag-waving tour leaders. On a low wall, a pair of old Muslim men sat and chatted together, oblivious to the crowd milling by. One man had a white wispy beard and the other had a pair of dark glasses that were far too big for him.

After I left the mosque, I found Joe and Rosie back at the hostel and we decided to go somewhere to eat. I brought them back to the Muslim Quarter where I had earlier seen some interesting restaurants. The streets were busy with people and lined with stalls selling a large assortment of snacks. After trying a few tasty nibbles, we opted for something more substantial. We walked into a nearby restaurant and were seated swiftly. The place was crowded, which is always a good sign. The walls were dotted with pictures of famous Chinese people eating and looking happy. The waiter offered us various small dishes containing plum pieces, vegetables, and spices. We agreed to order a selection of these food baskets and share them between us. Wicker baskets of mutton, beef, and vegetable dumplings arrived at our table at a steady rate. The dumplings were delicious and I was stuffed after ordering nine baskets.

ॐ

The sun was barely visible the following morning through the incredibly thick smog. It was my last day in Xian and I wanted to walk on the grand walls that surround the city. Xian's ramparts are rare as most city walls were destroyed during the Cultural Revolution. I accessed the walls via some stairs near the South Gate. From the top, the wall was as wide as the main streets below, and people used bicycles and motorized buggies to navigate its length. Xian's city walls are over thirteen kilometres long and a marathon is run on it every year.

I walked along the wall and squinted at the bare outline of the city through the smog. The walls were over seven hundred years old and had been started when Xian rivalled Rome as the greatest city on earth. Each ancient watchtower along the way had been thoughtfully converted into a souvenir shop or calligraphy store. It was a novel experience to be walking on the mighty walls of an ancient city but after thirty minutes, it just got monotonous and boring. Much of old Xian had been torn down by now so, as the writer Colin Thobrun noted, the walls were like the armour casing for a soldier who has long since passed away.

Suddenly, I heard singing. I leaned over the outside of the wall and saw a group of people below me playing instruments and singing. I decided to go down to get a closer look. When I got there, I saw that there were four musicians and two singers. The singing had a very strange and unusual high-pitched sound. A local girl came over to me and explained that this was Shaanxi Opera. The group met every Sunday morning to play their instruments and sing the traditional music of the province. I was delighted to be able to see such an authentic display of local music.

I left the musicians and joined Joe and Rosie back at the hostel. They were taking the train south towards Hong Kong that evening. It was to be our last evening of a short but very enjoyable time together. This is the nature of meeting people on the road. You meet people, become friends, and share a short part of your common journey together before parting ways.

"Here," Rosie said, taking off her big down jacket and thrusting it into my hands. "You'll need this more that I will." I tried to refuse her kindness but she wouldn't take it back. I thanked her profusely. It would prove to be a lifesaver later in my journey. It had been great to travel with such friendly people and we promised to keep in touch. Now, it was time for me to start on the road westwards and into a totally new culture.

7

INTO THE WEST

Lanzhou looked like a city that wouldn't be able to delay me for long. I had arrived in there after an uneventful overnight train from Xian. The train station backed onto a high cliff face and it seemed that the entire city was hemmed into a narrow valley through which flowed the Yellow River. Smog cloaked the town in darkness as I walked from the train station. The bare outline of industrial chimneys and bleak high-rise buildings poked through the haze. Blackish drops of rain smattered my coat by the time I found refuge in the nearest hotel.

Despite that, I was excited. Lanzhou was at the edge of the Tibetan world and an exciting new culture lay just beyond. I shared a lift with a few Tibetans to the upper floors of the hotel. They wore big beige cowboy hats and huge heavy coats with daggers stuck inside their belts. At one floor, the lift stopped and three Chinese soldiers joined us. The remainder of the journey in the lift seemed to last ages as both sides regarded each other with icy stares with me stuck in the middle. I spent the rest of the day catching up on some reading and just relaxing in my room. I had another long journey ahead of me the following

Monks resting on the steps of the main temple in Labrang

Pilgrims prostrating at Labrang

day.

Lanzhou bus station heaved with activity when I got there early the next morning. I took one look at the crowds bellowing and pushing at the ticket booth and sighed heavily. I forced my way through and, after some shouting and pointing, emerged clutching a bus ticket to Xiahe. The predominantly Tibetan town of Xiahe is home to the famous monastery of Labrang, one of the most important in Tibetan Buddhism. The ticket inspector showed me to a large mini-bus waiting in the yard. I asked him how long the journey would take and he informed me that it would take no more than four hours. Using my Chinese journey rule, I prepared myself for a five or six hour ride. I hadn't eaten any breakfast at that stage and felt hungry, but I couldn't see any of the usual food stalls that are normally found in a Chinese bus station. I decided to wait and prayed that we'd stop somewhere on the way. The bus filled quickly and after the driver finished his last breakfast cigarette, we were ready to go. As the bus pulled out of the station, I saw banks of noodle stalls that had been hidden by a line of parked buses. My last view of Lanzhou station was of people sitting at tables, happily eating steaming bowls of food as my stomach rumbled with hunger.

Lanzhou and Xiahe are both in the province of Gansu. It was a place where the Chinese had been sending their troublemakers since the days of the Emperor. The land outside Lanzhou was scorched and devoid of life. The distant hills and valleys seemed to be one mass of brittle and useless dust. Barren valleys and gullies were slashed across the land like axe marks on wood. It seemed like a terrible place to live.

The bus slowed through a small village where a market was taking place. There didn't seem to be anything other than leaks and cabbages for sale. The roofs of the passing houses were golden yellow with ears of corn drying under the morning sun. On a few roofs, satellite dishes cropped up between the ears of corn. Muslim men tended small flocks of sheep at the side of the

71

road and I spotted a camel tethered to a post behind a house as we sped by. This reminded me that the towns along this road were once important outposts on the famous Silk Route.

Linxia was once such a place. As we approached it, it seemed to have more in common with the Middle East than China. The town's skyline was dominated by a prominent mosque with a green, onion-shaped, dome, flanked by two green minarets. Crowds of Muslim men wearing white caps milled along the street after Friday prayers. Old wizened men with long white wispy beards sat holding tiny children outside their homes. They stared impassively at our bus as we passed by.

After Linxia, we descended into a valley split by a roaring river. I noticed signs that we were entering the Tibetan world. Buddhist monuments called *stupas* were dotted along the road. A *stupa* usually contains the relics or ashes of a Buddhist saint. Road signs appeared in both Chinese and Tibetan. Tibetan men walked by wearing the thick traditional coat called a *chuba*. Even though we were still in China, Tibetans were in the majority here. This area was historically part of the Tibetan province of Amdo. After China's invasion of Tibet in 1950, the province was assimilated into China. The bus pulled into the station in Xiahe an hour later. A few touts pointed excitedly at the lone foreigner behind the bus window. I sighed and got myself ready for bargaining.

I managed to bargain one tractor taxi driver down from five Yuan to three Yuan for the ride to my guesthouse. This bargaining over tiny amounts was a face-saving exercise for me. As a foreigner, I was going to be charged more than local people were, but as long as I was able to get the amount reduced, I had saved face. There was no public transport available in Xiahe, just the taxis and tractors that carried people along the main street. My tractor dropped me at the Tara Guesthouse and I booked into an otherwise empty dorm room. It seemed that I was the only guest at Tara and, for a while, I toyed with the idea that I may be the only foreigner in town.

I was famished after the long journey without any food so I went in search of something to eat. Xiahe is nearly three thousand meters above sea level so I found walking around a struggle at times. I spotted a restaurant above a souvenir shop on the main street. This was where all the restaurants were located, I guessed to avoid the dust of the streets. I climbed the grimy stairwell and sat at a plastic table on the balcony. The menu was in English and had an assortment of unfamiliar Tibetan dishes. I chanced a plate of Tibetan meat momos.

As I waited for my momos, I watched people on the street below. Groups of Tibetan monks in maroon robes walked along the streets doing some shopping. Old Muslim men with their white hats and long white beards stared at some products in a shop window. Tibetan nomads moved wearily along the street, clad in their heavy chubas and with their daggers tucked under their belts. Some of the older nomads wore huge dark glasses that looked like they were purchased in a joke shop. The Tibetan women looked uncomfortable in their multiple layers of clothing. The momos arrived which turned out to be just like dumplings, only meatier. A blind woman beggar entered the restaurant and stopped at each table, her outstretched hand clutching a bunch of filthy and tattered Chinese notes. She was ragged and almost toothless. She was the most wrenched person I'd ever seen. When she came to me, I pressed some notes into her hand and was rewarded with the warmest smile I had seen in a long time.

Even though it was quiet warm during the day, the temperature plummeted at night. At the guesthouse, hot water was only available from six to ten in the evening so I took the opportunity to wash up. Afterwards, I knocked on the door of the kitchen looking for hot water for my tea, and discovered there was another Western guest there, warming herself by a roaring fire. The family invited me in and a welcome bowl of steaming

Tibetan noodles was thrust into my cold hands. Janet didn't betray her seventy years and looked fresh and alert. She was in Xiahe researching Tibetan customs on behalf of her son. She told me that she'd spent four years in Amdo in Western Tibet and was staying at Tara Guesthouse until Christmas. She turned out to be a mine of information about the life of monks at Labrang. I basked in the glow of the open fire and enjoyed our conversation. An old Tibetan woman also sat by the fire twirling her prayer wheel, her face wrinkled and blackened with age.

Janet suggested that I visit to a Tibetan restaurant called Gesar, just across the road from the guesthouse. Gesar stayed open after nine at night, by which time all other places seemed to shut. I entered the small dining area where four Tibetan nomads and two monks sat watching Tibetan music videos. I saluted them with a loud *Tashi Dele* (Tibetan for Hello) as I entered and they all replied in kind. I intended to eat light so I ordered tofu and noodle soup with jasmine tea. I can't begin tell you how unsettling it is to have six Tibetans watch you eat in stony silence. Even when I took my head up from my meal to acknowledge one of their prolonged stares, they would only offer a quick smile before continuing to gawk at me, as if watching me eat some soup offered better entertainment that the Tibetan videos. I tried to break the silence by singing a verse of the Irish song *The Green Fields of France*, just to get a reaction. When I finished, one of the nomads seemed so surprised that he dropped his cup to the floor, smashing it to pieces. Nobody else uttered a word. I paid my bill quickly and was out the door like a shot, leaving the growing chatter of Tibetan in my wake.

ༀ

I ambled up the dusty road that led to Labrang monastery the following morning. This was one of the largest Tibetan monasteries outside Tibet itself. I joined a tour of the monastery, which had just started. The guide was a serious, red-faced monk who glared at me for joining the group so late. Despite this, he continued to lead the small group swiftly through the various monastery halls and museums, giving a cursory explanation of each room as he flew through them. It seemed as if our monk guide was in a rush to be somewhere else. We visited a room that contained some marvellous examples of yak-butter statues. Yak-butter is made from yak's milk and is a staple food in Tibetan areas. The statues were carefully crafted from this butter and can take weeks of meticulous work to make. Despite the effort and detail that goes into their creation, they eventually melt in the heat of summer. The creation and destruction of these statues expounds the Buddhist belief that inspired the intricate but temporary sand mandalas that can be seen in many Buddhist monasteries. It is the belief in the impermanence of things and how everything, even the most beautiful and intricate creations, will eventually disappear.

The monk guide then continued the whirlwind tour and led us outside. Small groups of monks sat in the doorways of houses, laughing and joking with each other. Some chattered into mobile phones like businessmen. One young novice monk was engrossed in a Game Boy, surrounded by his friends straining to see the action. We were then led to a courtyard to witness a scene that I didn't think I'd see until later in my trip. Young monks debated with each other while sitting cross-legged on the ground. Senior monks walked among them, correcting their arguments. Some of the young monks stood up and made their point with wild gesticulations before clapping their hands together to pass the right of reply back to their opponent.

"This help young monk remember better," explained the guide, jabbing his forehead with his finger. "When the monk think, then he understand better. The young boys can study here until the age of twenty," our guide continued. "Then, they must choose to continue as a monk or leave to make a life on the outside."

The monastery provides an education to those who cannot afford to go to public schools. Students can qualify to attend Labrang by first excelling at a local monastery. In that way, Labrang can be likened to famous Western colleges like Harvard or Oxford.

After the debating, we entered the courtyard of the main hall where monks were starting to congregate. Labrang is the seat of the Gelukpa sect, one of the four main schools of Tibetan Buddhism. They are known as the Yellow Hat sect due to the bright yellow hats they wear. On top of the main building, monks blew two huge gilded horns that were about eight feet long. The roar of the horns echoed across the valley. Other monks rang bells and burned juniper in a white chimney unit in the courtyard. Fragrant smoke wafted across in the air as pilgrims prayed and prostrated themselves before the main building. I was mesmerised. These were sights and sounds from another age. It was almost as if I'd been transported back in time. The horns sounded again and the monks shuffled into the main building.

"Now I go," declared our guide, clasping his hands together, and pressing them towards his forehead. His stony face finally broke into a beaming smile. He tossed his maroon cloak across his shoulder with a flourish and bounded up the steps of the hall. A couple of late arrivals sprinted up the steps after the main group, adjusting their yellow hats as they went. Some of the tour group followed the monks into the hall but I left to join the other pilgrims in doing the religious circuit around the monastery called the kora.

All over the Tibetan world, pilgrims perform the kora around religious buildings or stupas. There are nearly two thousand prayer wheels around the Labrang kora route and not one of them remains stationary during daylight hours. Each wheel contains scrolls of prayers and spinning the wheel is supposed to send those prayers towards the heavens. The procession of people, the chanting, and the constant twirling of prayer wheels is an experience in itself. The pilgrims fingered their prayer beads with one hand while spinning wheels with the other. Everybody moved with purpose in a clockwise direction, muttering the manta *Omni padme hum*. This mantra roughly translates to *hail the jewel in the flower of the lotus*. Most wore big *chubas* with one sleeve off the shoulder. Others wore them tied around their waists.

As I followed the pilgrims around, I spotted a woman ahead of me prostrating full-length on the ground. She rose from the dust and clasped her hands to her forehead, lips, and chest before again going full length on her stomach. Only a leather apron and gloves protected her skin. She moved herself forward slowly, repeating a mantra before prostrating herself once more. I watched her for a few minutes in a state of awe. The religious zeal required to do that must be amazing.

I left the main monastery complex and went to investigate a gilded stupa near the river that I'd seen earlier. As I was paying my entrance fee to the stupa, a man started chatting to me about my visit. At first, I thought he was a tour guide looking for business so I tried to excuse myself politely.

"Don't worry my friend," he assured me. "I want to show you this place for no money."

Frank was a Tibetan from Xining, the capital city of the neighbouring province of Qinghai. He spoke excellent English and was fluent in Chinese. He told me that he was in Xiahe doing research for the University of Xining. After we had climbed the wooden stairs of the stupa, he explained that this was where the bones of Labrang's founder were entombed. He was an expert about the monastery and its surroundings. He offered to show me around other parts of Labrang and I readily accepted.

As we walked back to the monastery, he talked about the importance of Labrang.

"Labrang is like a western university, with its own colleges of astrology, traditional medicine, theology," Frank explained. "There are over sixty thousand Buddhist books and sutras stored in the monastery so it's a place of great knowledge and learning. Over four and a half thousand monks are enrolled to study here but only about four hundred are full-time. There are hundreds more waiting for the chance to learn at such a prestigious place."

I replied that it must be a good sign that so many monks are coming to Labrang. However, Frank shook his head ruefully.

"The Chinese government has imposed a limit on the number of students the monastery can accept and every one of them has to carry a special identity card. This angers the people," he admitted.

I asked Frank about the woman I had seen prostrating around Labrang earlier.

"Yes, many pilgrims choose to do the kora this way. It takes about eight hours to complete the circuit of the monastery in this fashion but the pilgrim is happy to do this. I have seen many pilgrims who prostrate themselves all the way to Lhasa from their villages in Tibet."

"And how long would that take?" I asked.

"Not longer than one or two years," he replied nonchalantly.

It seemed that one of the main wishes of the Tibetans is for religious freedom, without any external controls. Frank never said it but I sensed that this was the freedom they craved, instead of the political one. Without religion, there is no Tibet.

Frank brought me to the College of Medicine where we watched students reciting lists of herbs, learning by heart which herbs are best for each particular ailment. Like Chinese medicine, Tibetan medicine is herbal based and goes back over four thousand years. Frank then led me to a courtyard and showed me the houses of the forty incarnate lamas who reside at Labrang. A lama is a Tibetan Buddhist teacher. Tibetans believe in reincarnation so that once a person dies, their spirit is reborn in the body of a baby. In the case of important lamas, once they pass away, the senior monks work quickly to find and identify the child into which the spirit has gone to and appoint that child the new lama-in-waiting. At Labrang, the most senior of these was a four-year-old boy, believed to be the incarnation of the founder of Labrang.

In addition to the College of Medicine, Frank also wanted to show me the College of Astrology. He believed that the senior lamas at this college could do some remarkable things based on ancient Tibetan knowledge. When I pressed him on this, he told me stories of lamas being seen in different places at the same time, and of others levitating into the air. He said that he himself had seen one lama rise into the air while being turned into a brilliant light. When we reached the entrance of the college, a monk approached us and told Frank that no Westerners were allowed inside. Frank managed to convince him that I was a student of his and he let us pass.

We entered the College of Astrology through heavy maroon curtains. Yak-butter lamps cast a dim light around the hall and the smell of burning butter filled the air. It took a few minutes for my eyes to adjust to the darkness. I then made out rows of hooded monks sitting cross-legged on the floor. The walls echoed with their deep chanting like the collective hum of bees. A menacing looking character walked amongst them as they swayed back and forth. He wore a huge cape, draped across his shoulders on some sort of frame that made him look twice as broad as he was. He moved around the hall silently, as if he were gliding on air. The hall had an unearthly feel to it and I was convinced that once Frank and I left, the whole class levitated off the ground to their normal position.

Frank told me that he had to leave to catch his bus back to Xining. I walked with him towards the bus station. As we parted, I thanked him for his help.

"Here," he said. "I have something for you." He reached inside his coat and produced a small yellow satchel with a shoulder strap.

"Please, this is for you." The small bag was made of course wool and had a strange symbol on it. I asked him what it was.

"This is a very holy Buddhist symbol called Om," he explained. "It is full of meaning. It is a very good symbol to display in Tibet." I thanked him and waved him off as he left for the bus station.

On the way back to the hostel, I popped into an internet café to check my e-mail. Young novice monks played games of Quake and Doom on the computers, blasting away at each other with a deafening roar. A German tourist seated himself next to me and introduced himself as Fritz. Sorry, that's not his real name but I can't remember what it was. For some reason, I took an instant dislike to him.

"How long will you be staying here?" he asked me. I told him I was planning to leave the following day.

"Then you will miss the festival that is happening in the town. What a shame," he informed me with obvious glee. (I felt a little better when I later discovered it was a Festival of Silence).

Since I had left Xian, I had decided to try to enter Tibet illegally. The Chinese authorities required that any foreigner entering Tibet must purchase an expensive tourist permit. It was a way for them to both cash in on the popularity of the region and monitor tourists. By not buying the permit, it would be my small way of giving the finger to the system. I told Fritz about my plans.

"A Swedish friend of mine also tried to do this but was caught and sent back. He had to buy the permit and fly to Tibet."

Fritz was now in full flow and boasting about what a smart boy he was to buy the permit and what a dope I was to attempt to get to Tibet illegally.

"I think that you should not try this," he advised. "The permit is not that expensive."

I left the internet café and walked back to the guesthouse in a bad mood. Fritz had poured a bucket of cold water on my hopes and I hated him for it. I hated him for his sensible suggestions and reasoning. However, it was hard to deny that trying to get into Tibet illegally was fraught with risk. The easiest way would be to do as he suggested and just buy the permit. As I packed my bags that night in readiness for my early morning departure, I decided to let fate guide me and take whatever path was presented to me.

The moon and stars were still visible when I left Tara Guesthouse the following morning. I hailed a tractor taxi on the street and bargained with the balaclava-clad driver to bring me to the bus station. The bus to Xining was the first to leave that morning so many of the food stalls had not opened yet. I made do with a pack of biscuits and a disgusting orange flavoured drink. I settled into my seat on the bus and glanced around at my travelling companions. Monks and Tibetan nomads chatted and dozed in their seats. We departed in total darkness just after six that morning. Seeing a place like Labrang was the reason I had started to travel in the first place. I was delighted to have seen such exotic ceremonies as I had the day before. It felt special to me and I hoped it would always remain as I had seen it. Change comes slowly to this remote part of the Tibetan world. I hope and pray that it takes all the time in the world.

8

AMONGST MUSLIMS

As we left the town of Xiahe behind, the bus climbed a steep and rough road out of the town. With its headlights beaming into the darkness, the bus rumbled up and down the broken road, swaying back and forth so wildly that I was convinced it would be overturned. However, the road soon levelled out and we found ourselves on a flat plain that stretched for miles into the horizon. These were the Sanke Grasslands, where nomads tended their yak herds during the summer months. The rising sun soon illuminated the rough but beautiful landscape. Narrow streams of smoke rose from the mud huts that were dotted along the road. The land was arid and poor and there was no doubt that life was hard for the people who made it their home.

It was going to be a long journey to Xining, the capital of the remote province of Qinghai in northwest China. As usual, I had been told that the journey would take about five hours so I knew it would be at least seven or eight. In China, bus passengers accept breakdowns, flat tyres, and other more unexplained delays without complaining. It's simply part of public transport in China and in much of Asia as well.

Tibetan procession in honour of the lama of Labrang

The Grand Mosque of Xining

The bus stopped outside a small house beside the road to pick up two old Tibetan men. The Chinese driver seemed to be in a foul mood and he berated them for taking so long to get aboard. They slowly made their way to two seats across from me. After they settled in, they noticed me reading my guidebook and were unable to hide their fascination. I offered it to them to browse through. Once the old men had it, people from other seats scrambled over to them to get a look. The old men assumed the role of guardians of the book and insisted that they alone would turn the pages and discuss its contents. The Tibetan-English section at the back of the book was a huge hit, but it was the sketch drawing of the Dali Lama that caused the biggest stir. The old men pressed his image to their foreheads and passed it to others to do the same. That page was pressed against many foreheads that day.

Three hours into the journey, the bus slowed due to an unusual amount of traffic on the road. Smoke billowed into the air and, at first, I thought a car had careered off the edge of the road and burst into flames. However, it turned out that some Tibetans were burning a huge fire near the roadside. I asked one of the passengers what was going on. He managed to communicate to me that the four-year-old incarnate Lama of Labrang, the one Frank had spoken about, was being driven around the local area. As the bus drove by the car containing the young lama, the two old men beside me took off their hats out of respect. They also threw small prayer papers out the window, muttering a mantra as the papers fluttered into the wind.

A procession of Tibetan motorcyclists led the way for the lama's car and slowed our progress to a crawl. Their bikes were brightly decorated with flags, bunting, and flowers. Following closely behind them were truckloads of happy Tibetans, their vehicles bedecked with a kaleidoscope of coloured flags. It was a very joyous parade and everyone was in high spirits. A policeman ordered our bus to stop while the procession passed by.

There was a lot of shouting, singing, and whooping from the Tibetans in the trucks, making our Chinese driver even grumpier than before. At the villages that the procession passed through, the local people lined the sides of the road to sing and prostrate themselves in front of the lama's car. After about thirty minutes, we branched off the road and left the happy gathering behind as we headed for Xining.

I was relieved when we stopped at a small town for food, as I was starving. We piled into a restaurant and I ordered the safe option of noodle soup yet again. One of the old men from the bus insisted on paying for my soup and refused to take any money for it. To return the favour, I bought some oranges at the market and passed them around the bus later on.

I had been on the cramped bus for over eight hours when the city of Xining came into view. As I got off at the small bus station, a man approached me and introduced himself as Mr. Zhang. He quickly rattled off some well-versed story about the various merits of a hotel he knew and suggested that I should at least see the rooms. He seemed honest enough so I followed him across the bridge to the hotel. After examining the rooms, I opted for a bed in a clean dorm in which I was the only person.

Mr. Zhang referred to himself as the Information Officer and told me to ask him if I needed anything. I asked him if he knew where I could get some Eight Flavours Tea. I had discovered this extraordinary tea in Xiahe and had become addicted to it. The tea was sold in a small plastic sachet that contained flowers, herbs, green tea, and a piece of crystal sugar. Once you added boiling water to the mix, it looked like an underwater flowerbed with bright yellows, reds, and greens. Each sachet made about five or six cups of delicious tea. Mr. Zhang showed me to a nearby market where I bought some of the tea and a tea-flask. After I returned to my room, I relaxed after the long bus journey and enjoyed some sweet tea.

Mr. Zhang mentioned something to me on the way to the

hotel that intrigued me. He said it was possible to get a sleeper bus direct from Xining to Lhasa, the capital of Tibet. That possibility wasn't mentioned in my guidebook. When I asked him if foreigners were allowed to take the bus, he lowered his voice and became comically secretive.

"If you pay driver, then he take you, no problem."

This could be my way of getting into Tibet, I thought. It was definitely something for me to think about.

ॐ౦ॐ

The Great Mosque of Xining is indeed worthy of the name. Two tall minaret towers rose on either side of a green, onion-shaped dome. Two blue Chinese style towers stood at either end of the façade. Some fake palm had been erected outside the main entrance and gave the Mosque a distinctively Arabic feel. Inside the main entrance was a huge courtyard, crowded with Muslim men wearing their distinctive white hats. I felt a little uneasy as I sensed people looking at me. After the bad press surrounding Muslims and the events of 9/11, it was hard to know how they would react to me. Soon, a man approached me and spoke to me in English. He asked me the usual questions about where I was from and how did I like Xining.

"Are there Muslim people in your country," he asked. I told him that there were many Muslims from all over the world working in Ireland. Soon, a crowd had gathered around us. They listened intently as the man translated my answers for them. Some of them asked him questions that they wanted me to answer.

"Some people want to know why President Bush is so hard on the Muslims," he said.

That was a tough one. I tried to explain as best I could but I wasn't making sense. It was not easy to explain.

A bell rang and the crowd quickly made for the prayer hall, saying their goodbyes to me as they left. It was a remarkable transformation as the courtyard was packed only a minute earlier. The men kicked off their shoes in scattered piles outside the prayer hall before entering. A few latecomers rushed by me on their way to prayer. I watched the men inside bowing low to the ground in response to the Imam's (Muslim priest) chants. The prayers only lasted about fifteen minutes, after which the people filed out again to resume their daily lives.

I wandered back to my room in the hotel. I'd barely settled on my bed when there was a knock on the door. Mr. Zhang had come to tell me about all the sights that I could see around Xining if I was interested. I thanked him but told him I was much more interested in going somewhere to eat.

"I know a very good place," he said. He insisted on accompanying me to the restaurant. It was a nice spot and we shared it with a table of drunken Chinese truck drivers. Once I sat down, the attention of the drivers was diverted towards me. I wasn't planning on drinking so I tried to ignore the chorus of Hellos that was coming from their table. One of them staggered over to me, bottle of baijiu in his hand, intent that I drink it with him. I tried to ignore him but he was very persistent. He said something to me that Mr. Zhang translated.

"He said may both of us be happy and may this drink be the start of our friendship."

How could I ignore that? Details of the night are a bit fuzzy after that point but I do remember that we spent the night trying to out-drink and out-toast each other. One of the truck drivers got to his feet and announced that the already well-lit restaurant was further illuminated when I entered it. I don't know how they came up with that stuff. Not to be out-done, I stood up and, with a sloshing glass of rice wine in my hand, answered that China need not worry about economic riches when it had its real treasure in people like these drivers. Mr. Zhang translated and the drivers nearly started sobbing. After a night of drinking baijiu, bear hugging, and invites to Ireland, I staggered back to the hotel.

I got up at a respectable hour despite the impromptu party the night before. I'd hardly made my first cup of tea before Mr. Zhang was knocking on my door. He closed the door behind him and sat on the bed. He didn't waste any time getting down to business.

"It may be possible to take you on the bus that is leaving for Lhasa today," he announced. He lowered his voice slightly and leaned towards me.

"The driver wants eight hundred Yuan for this. Is this acceptable for you?"

This was the opportunity I had been waiting for. It made the gruelling thirty-two hour bus journey to Lhasa just about worth it. He was offering me a way into Tibet on my terms and I took it.

"You pay two hundred for the ticket now," he said, writing the ticket out in front of me.

"You pay the rest to the driver. This way, you can get to Tibet without need for permit".

He ripped off the ticket stub with a flourish and presented it to me. I could hardly contain my excitement. I was going to Tibet.

9

HIGH ROAD TO TIBET

The bus driver was like a character from a Chinese gangster film. A cigarette dangled from the corner of his mouth, the cigarette smoke nearly obscuring his face. Acne scars pocketed his face, and he wore a bitter expression that suggested he had been breast-fed by his father. A pair of dark sunglasses hoarded his eyes and completed the gangster look. Mr. Zhang climbed up to his cab and had a whispered conversation with him before I was beckoned to come aboard.

"You pay the driver now," he said to me quietly.

I produced the envelope from my jacket and handed it to the driver. He opened it quickly and fingered the notes inside. The driver grunted something and Mr. Zhang left the bus.

"Driver will take care of everything now," he explained as he waved goodbye to me and walked away quickly. I prayed he was right.

I gave my backpack to one of the driver's helpers and he put in the luggage bay of the bus. I climbed aboard the bus and the driver pointed me towards the back. The Tibetan passengers stared at me as I walked along the bus aisle. The bus was a

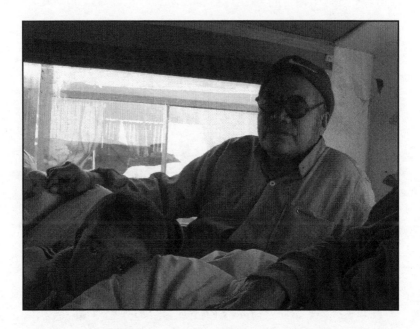

Some of my neighbours on the bus to Lhasa

The barren wastelands of northern Tibet

large, sleeper type and had two rows of bunks that ran from front to back. The bunks could double as seating during the day. The driver pointed me to a large sleeping area in the back of the bus. It was roughly the size of a double bed and there was plenty of room for me to stretch out on. It seemed luxurious when compared to the cramped seating the other passengers had to endure. I reckoned I deserved the extra space considering what I had paid. I would soon find out how wrong I would be.

The bus departed from the city centre soon after but stopped at regular intervals in the suburbs to pick up more passengers. At one stop, two old Tibetan nomads got on and only had eyes for the empty space on either side of me. Once they had settled in, their wives and children joined them so I ended up crushed between six people. The elder nomad was a colourful character who wore a bright orange shirt and huge dark glasses. His skin was very dark, almost black and he wore a red hat with the Nike swoosh symbol. Everyone was wearing multiple layers of clothing to guard against the cold so we were like astronauts stuffed in the back of a spacecraft. The nomads themselves were friendly and full of smiles. The old nomad and his children were covered in so much wool that it seemed they hadn't been separated from their animals in a very long time. Every time I thought that we had taken on the last passenger the bus could handle, the driver would stop and pick up a few more. People occupied every available bit of space, including the floor. Once the driver was satisfied that the bus was dangerously over-crowded, he drove out of the city, leaving the bright lights of Xining behind.

I settled in as best I could and tried to make myself comfortable. I had brought along some books but I shouldn't have bothered as the road was too bumpy for reading. There was nothing to do but stare out the window at the passing land-scape. We only made one stop that night to go to the toilet and stock up on snacks. I had been advised to drink plenty of water on the journey but when the villainous driver only allowed us a few toilet breaks, it was a dangerous game to play with my bladder. As night fell, the temperature dropped and the windows froze. Being squeezed in between the heavily clothed nomads wasn't so bad after all as our combined body heat kept us all warm. A woolly nomad is all a man needs when he feels the cold. Even when I slept, I wore my jacket, cap, and socks so I was well insulated. However, with the extra passengers now occupying the back of the bus, room to sleep was severely limited. With my knees drawn up to my chest, I drifted into a fitful sleep as the bus rattled across China.

I awoke a number of times during the night to find that the bus had broken down. Each time, the driver opened the front cab and hammered loudly at the engine until it fired back to life again. This would become a regular sight for the duration of the journey.

I was awoken the following morning by my neighbours munching as breakfast officially commenced. The windows of the bus were still frozen and I couldn't see a thing through them. The rising sun soon started to thaw them and I began to make out the passing terrain. Far away in the distance, mountains rose out of the flat, lifeless plains and sand dunes appeared in the distance. The desert soon gave way to snow covered mountains and an even bleaker landscape. Within four hours, we reached Golmud.

As I looked around the barren outpost of a town, it was hard to disagree with my guidebook's description of Golmud as one of the most desolate towns imaginable. It seemed bleak and completely devoid of life. Wind swirled along the deserted streets, throwing up small flurries of snow. A dead dog lay on one of the many piles of dirty snow that lined the footpaths. I watched two army personnel, dressed in heavy coats, moving slowly along the icy street. They seemed to walk with apathy and resignation, and paid no attention to us or to anything else. I wondered what massive blunder they had committed to be posted here. It was surely a hardship location for the army or civil servants. I imagined they had a phrase in the government that went, 'He was sent to Golmud'. At any rate, we didn't have a long break there and we left the town without much delay.

We had just left Golmud when the bus stopped suddenly. I had been dozing next to the warm, woolly nomads and didn't see the border inspector board the bus. My neighbours reacted quickly and buried me in blankets to prevent me from being seen. The inspector seemingly made a cursory check around the bus and left quickly. That had taken me by surprise. The part of the journey that I had been dreading was just ahead. Mr. Zhang told me to expect two checkpoints before entering Tibet, one just after Golmud and one before the Tibet border. I remembered his promise about the driver taking care of things. Now, I wasn't so sure.

After an hour, the bus pulled over on the hard shoulder behind another bus. The driver ambled down the aisle to me and started blabbering away in Chinese. I looked at him blankly and uttered, "Ting boo dong," meaning, "I don't understand." He looked a bit taken aback by that. Maybe Mr. Zhang told him I spoke Chinese. He then produced a piece of paper and started writing Chinese characters on it. Did he actually expect me to read Chinese if I couldn't speak it? I said, "Can boo dong," which means, "I don't read Chinese." He looked ready to erupt with rage. His face cracked into a wicked smile as he started drawing a picture of a bus with the back door open. He then drew a stick figure standing next to the open door. He smiled his villainous smile and pointed at me, then to the stick figure. It finally dawned on me what he was trying to say. He wanted me to hide in the back of the bus. I couldn't believe it. First, I tried to refuse but I soon realised that there was no other way.

As I walked off the bus, the other passengers looked at me as if they'd never see me again. I remembered my backpack locked in the luggage bay of the bus but the driver just ushered me off quickly. I had a sick feeling in the pit of my stomach as we walked towards the second bus. The driver from that bus was waiting at the back of the vehicle. He opened the back door, placed a thin mattress on the floor, and motioned to me to climb inside. I did so even with every fibre of my being telling me not to. My driver pointed at his watch and held up ten fingers, informing me I should only be in there ten minutes. I didn't know what to believe at that stage. The door slammed shut and I was plunged into darkness. The bus moved off and I could hear the gears crunching as we picked up speed. I started to think of all the possible ways this could end. Was the driver going to rob me? Was he planning to kill me and steal my stuff? Was I going to be held for a ransom? After what seemed like an hour, the bus stopped again. I could hear voices talking outside and someone walking around the bus. I held my breath and barely blinked. Soon after, the bus started again and came to another halt about twenty minutes later. The door opened and the bright light of day flooded into my dark cell. I didn't know if I was going to see a stern-faced border guard or the barrel of a gun. Instead, it was my driver's hardened face that smiled down on me. I can tell you I was bloody delighted to see those pitiless features again. He extended his hand to help me out. As I got back on my old bus, the Tibetans smiled broadly and gave me the thumbs-up sign as if welcoming a lost son. I slumped back into my space between my neighbours, exhausted.

ༀ༄ༀ

During the rest of the journey that day, the vista changed

little. Howling winds, laden with snow, surged down from the slopes of towering mountains and whipped across the desolate plains below them. It was the most inhospitable terrain I had ever seen. The bus climbed higher towards the peaks that form the border with Tibet. There was little to do on the bus but sleep or try to look out the window at the blankness outside. At one point, the driver played a very raunchy DVD on the bus television of some scantily clad Chinese women pole dancing. I thought it was very out of place on a bus full of Tibetan pilgrims although no one seemed to object to it, least of all myself. In fact, I looked around and noticed the rows of eyes, both men and women, transfixed by the gyrating beauties on the flickering television screen. It seemed that the prayer beads had been put aside, momentarily at least. Any distraction on such a boring journey was more than welcome.

As we climbed higher into the mountains, I started to feel unwell and developed a thumping headache. There was nothing to do but lie back between the nomads and try to sleep. At some stage, we crossed the Tanggula Pass at over five thousand, two hundred metres high. I was finally in Tibet, the holy grail of my entire trip. I managed a weak smile despite my splitting headache.

Conditions at the back of the bus worsened. The initial novelty of having a Westerner on board quickly wore off for the Tibetans, and I was constantly being elbowed to make space, even though there wasn't any more room. I managed to wrestle the space back each time I lost it. My blankets had become filthy with breadcrumbs and a crushed banana. The old nomad next to me had a bad cough and had the lovely habit of turning in my direction when a particularly bad fit raked him. Despite those discomforts, I was only aware of the thumping pain in my head.

Darkness had fallen on my second night on the bus when we stopped at a basic-looking eatery outside a small town. The shack was built of corrugated iron and smelled of urine. As I got off the bus, I staggered a little, as if I had been drinking. I felt out-of-breath, light-headed, and had trouble focusing on objects. Inside the small restaurant, I tried unsuccessfully to eat some noodles. I didn't have any appetite for food so I just climbed back on the bus to rest.

Looking back on it, these are all classic symptoms of mountain sickness. This is a common complaint when people travel into altitude faster than their body can adjust. Mild cases can result in headaches and feeling unwell. More severe cases at high altitudes can lead to fluid build-up in the lungs or brain and, ultimately, death. After the bus departed, I lay back and tried to sleep. I had no idea how far we were from Lhasa. At that stage, all I wanted was to be off the bus and into a hot shower and a clean bed. The journey was quickly turning into a nightmare.

At some unknown time during the night, the bus stopped for the umpteenth time. The windows were frozen again so I couldn't see where we were. Normally, the bus would depart again after the driver had managed to get the engine going but this time, we were stationary for over an hour. I stepped over the body of the sleeping driver and got off the bus. A blast of wind knocked the breath out of me. I'd never experienced cold like it before. I could see a convoy of buses and trucks, parked bumper to bumper to the back and front of our bus. It seemed that we had stopped for the night. I went behind the bus and got sick.

In the distance, I could see the lights of a town or city. Were they the lights of Lhasa, I wondered? Could we really be that close? I saw taxis ferrying people from the buses and trucks towards the city. I became convinced that it was indeed Lhasa. The promise of a hot shower and warm bed lay with those bright city lights and I was willing to pay hundreds of Yuan to get there. I decided there and then to make a break for it. I climbed back on the bus and tried to wake the sleeping driver so I could get my bag out of the luggage bay. He just waved me off and went back to sleep. I continued to rock his shoulders and shout at him that I wanted my bag. Another night on that bus would have been hell. I managed to stop a taxi and explain that I wanted to go to Lhasa. He left the car to help me get my backpack. Together, we pummelled the driver until he woke up. I pointed at the distant lights.

"Lhasa, Lhasa," I shouted, my voice filled with desperation.

The driver shook his head.

"Lhasa, no. Nagqu, Nagqu," he shouted and went back to sleep. My heart sank. That wasn't Lhasa at all but a small town about three hundred kilometres north of it. I was crestfallen. I had to spend another night on the bus. The taxi driver left and I managed to regain my spot between the smelly nomads. I fell into an exhausted sleep.

I awoke the following morning to a foul smell hitting my nostrils. The face of my sleeping neighbour was plastered to mine, and his stinking breath reeked of meals consumed days ago. The windows were frozen yet again, denying me a view of the outside world. We had been on the move since early that morning. My headache had receded and I felt a little better. Barring a disaster, we would arrive in Lhasa that day.

I gave up trying to figure out how far we had to go and just wallowed in apathy. Once the windows thawed, I sat back and stared blankly at the passing countryside. Along the route I saw Tibetan houses, whose walls were peppered with cakes of yak dung. Once the dung dries, it is used for fuel. Herds of yak along with sheep and horses roamed the wastes, some with colourful ribbons tied to their tails. Every village along the route looked as if it were recovering from a war. It was a desperate looking part of the world.

I was dozing when a sudden thump brought the bus to a shuddering halt. Everyone looked out the window to see what had happened. The bus had crashed into a truck coming in the opposite direction. I don't know how it happened as we were going very slowly at the time. Everyone left the bus to inspect the damage, which wasn't very serious. The two drivers argued heatedly about who was to blame for the accident. A small crowd gathered around the drivers to watch the show. As they both raged at each other, the rest of us took the opportunity to stretch our legs and wash in a nearby stream. I went across the road and sat on the bank of the stream, enjoying the warm sun on my face. In the distance, workers swung picks and hammers as they laboured on a railway bridge. I guessed that this was part of the railway to Lhasa.

The proposed railway link to Lhasa had posed some unique problems that the Chinese were determined to solve. Swiss engineers had declared that it was impossible to build a railway to Lhasa due to the unstable nature of the permafrost they would have to build on. This only made the Chinese authorities more determined to prove the Westerners wrong. Chinese engineers dealt with this problem by building elevated tracks with the foundations sunk deep into the ground and building hollow concrete pipes beneath the tracks to keep the rail bed frozen. There were also plans to build a series of hospitals along the line to treat potential cases of altitude sickness.

We filed back onto the bus past the dejected looking figure of the bus driver. It seemed that he had been blamed for the accident, which was about right as far as I could see. It couldn't have happened to a nicer guy. I only hope he had to give most of my six hundred Yuan to the other driver.

As the journey wore on, I spotted signs that we were approaching a major city. Power lines, construction plants, horticultural centres, and improved roads were indications that Lhasa was near. The Tibetans must have known this as well because they started to sing and my spirits soared with theirs. I even sang a verse of *You All Smell but I Don't Care*, a little ditty that I'd composed in one of my more bored moments on the bus. Even the driver's brutal face cracked a little smile as he probably thought of the beer and hookers he was going to enjoy.

Finally, gloriously, I saw the 'Welcome to Lhasa' sign. What a beautiful sign, a wonderful, blessed sign. After a few more twists and turns, we arrived at Lhasa Bus Station. Everyone piled off the bus and wasted little time in going their separate ways. I didn't even have time to say goodbye to my neighbours. I hailed a taxi and told the driver to bring me to the highly recommended Yak Hotel.

As the taxi sped through Lhasa, we rounded a corner and the Potala appeared on my left. The Potala was the former residence of the Dali Lama and a symbol of Tibet. What a sight it was on such a lovely, sunny day. I didn't want to look at it too much. I wanted to save it for later so I could really enjoy the view I had waited so long to see. I sat back and sighed heavily. I'd made it! I was in Lhasa. I felt a real sense of achievement. I had reached one of the highest cities in the world by bus. It had been tough going but it was worth it. In ways, the ordeal of the bus journey made my arrival in the city all the sweeter. I had *earned* the right to be here and to see the famous Potala. I thought of the Tibetan pilgrims who prostrate themselves around monasteries for hours and I felt I understood why they did that a little better. Finally, I thought of Fritz, the German who had told me not to try to enter Tibet illegally. I smiled and gave him a mental middle finger.

10

LHASA

The prayer wheel in the old woman's hand squeaked like an old bicycle as she turned it. A small bead hung off the turning head of the wheel so it looked almost like a child's toy when in motion. Studs of red and blue glass lined the outside of the wheel, making it look more expensive than it probably was. It had doubtless sent many thousands of prayers towards the heavens. The old woman deftly counted out the beads in her left hand and she turned the wheel in the other hand, chanting prayers to herself. Thousands of other pilgrims just like her, gathered in the city to pay homage and turn their prayer wheels. This is why I had come to Lhasa.

After my epic bus journey from China, I had planned to relax for a day. However, the prospect of seeing the Potala was too exciting to stay indoors. Once I got to the end of the main street, the gigantic building came into view and held me transfixed. The sides of the Potala sloped inwards right up to the very top. It looked like a pyramid without the pointed apex. The building is almost entirely white except for the maroon coloured top portion, which was the former residence of the Dali Lama.

Pilgrims prostrating before the Potala in Lhasa

Monks debating scripture at Sera Monastery

Windows only started to appear halfway up its cliff-like sides. Maroon-coloured steps led up from both sides of the building and doubled back on themselves on their way to the top. Set against an impossibly blue sky with white wispy clouds, I had no trouble believing that it could have once housed a God.

After I enjoyed the view from the outside, I wanted to see what it was like inside. I climbed the steep steps upwards to the entrance. The Potala is under constant renovation and only a tiny number of its one thousand rooms are open to the public. Tourists are required to enter the Potala from the back of the building, so that they and the Tibetan pilgrims go in opposite directions for security reasons. As I moved about the building, I noticed security cameras on the ceilings of most of the rooms and chapels. The Chinese were keen to keep a close eye on all activities within the walls of the Potala, a symbol of Tibetan freedom. As I investigated one particular chapel, a monk approached me.

"Where are you from?" he asked me.

"Ireland," I answered.

"Ah, this is very good. Your country has helped Tibet much in the past."

I asked him what he meant.

"In a debate in United Nations, Ireland was one of only a small number of countries to protest the invasion by China. This was very brave." I had not known about that myself. He noticed the guidebook under my arm.

"The history of Tibet in this book is very good, not mixed up like the Chinese have made it." I was a little amazed by his frankness and I couldn't help glancing up nervously at the security camera on the ceiling. After exploring a few more rooms, I went onto the roof of the Potala and admired the fine view of the city and the surrounding mountains. Despite that, it did little to dispel my feeling of disappointment. What had once been the living, breathing heart of Tibet now felt empty and vacant.

Ancient corridors that once echoed and hummed with prayer and crashing cymbals were now silent. The spiritual heart of the Potala was gone and that was what mattered most.

After I left the Potala, I decided to treat myself to a good lunch. I entered the empty Tashi Restaurant through chequered curtains. Three Tibetan girls jumped up from some books they were reading and showed me to a table. I ordered an omelette, tea, and yogurt. Once I had my food, the girls returned to their study. I realised they were learning English so I offered to help them in exchange for a few lessons in Tibetan. They were very keen to learn and had little trouble picking up the basic sentences I taught them. Conversely, they were soon laughing hard at my attempts to pronounce simple Tibetan phrases.

In the middle of the lesson, a group of four tourists came in. I hadn't spoken to another Westerner in a week, so I joined them at their table for a chat. Walter was a fresh-faced Canadian who had linked up with the group in China. Ameldine and Claire were two French girls travelling through Asia after finishing their studies in France.

"Where in Ireland are you from?" asked Caroline, who had been silent up to this point. She told me she was from Co. Kerry in Ireland and had just completed her acupuncture studies in Nanjing before taking time to travel in Tibet. Caroline was an attractive brunette with pale, clear skin, and kind blue eyes. When she smiled, small dimples appeared on the sides of her face. Her long brown hair hung down to her shoulders and she wore a nose-stud of a small dragonfly. We fell into our own private conversation as the others ordered food. We talked about our travels and joked easily. It was nice to meet another Irish traveller and talk about home.

"I'm going to have a look around Barkhor Square if anyone would like to come with me?" I asked after we had finished our meals.

"Yea, I'll go along with you," Caroline replied, much to my delight.

We left the restaurant and walked the short distance to Barkhor Square, the religious focal point of Lhasa. In the middle of the square is the Jokhang, the holiest temple in Tibet. Pilgrims come from the remotest corners of the Tibetan world to visit the Jokhang and to do the Barkhor Kora, the religious circuit around the temple. Caroline and I joined the pilgrims as they walked along the kora route around the temple. Stalls selling a vast array of religious goods lined the sacred route almost without interruption. This was where the business of religion was at its fiercest. Among the items for sale were animal furs, wooden masks of fearsome demons, huge necklaces made from yak bone as big as grapes, cymbals, gilded cow heads, and even Christian crucifixes. Prayer flags were available in an explosion of colours and rows of prayer wheels stood upright, like soldiers in neat rows.

Pilgrims chanted and twirled their prayer wheels as they walked around the Jokhang. Two Tibetan men paused from their prayers to talk with us. One wore rose-tinted glasses and a Chinese style coat while his friend sported a McDonalds top and a fur hat made from an entire fox skin, complete with head and feet. Another pilgrim approached soon afterwards wearing red tassels in his hair and a bright luminous green vest. His gold teeth shone when he smiled.

On our way around, we saw a man prostrating himself on the ground as he completed the kora. He wore protective leather pads on his arms and wooden blocks on his hands. He raised his hands together above his head before touching them to his forehead, lips, and chest and then going full stretch on the ground. I was told he would repeat this for the entire day. A huge callus on his forehead told the story of the many thousands of times his head had touched the ground in devotion. A young child dressed in rags walked beside him and held out a can begging for alms.

It was awesome to see the religious fervour of the Tibetan people. In front of the Jokhang, the pilgrims have worn the rough ground smooth from their years of prostrating. They wore pieces of cardboard on their hands and knees for protection as they repeatedly throw themselves full-length on the ground. There were about thirty people prostrating that morning and together they made a sound like rushing water. On the roof of the Jokhang, a golden wheel with two deer kneeling on either side of it gleamed in the sun. We wanted to go inside the temple but were told that it was closed that day. We decided to return another time.

After the Barkhor, Caroline returned to her hotel to rest after her flight and I went back to the Yak Hotel. My dorm room was comfortable and clean, with the added bonus of excellent hot showers. To say I enjoyed the hot shower after my long bus journey from Xining would only be to hint at the shear joy I felt. They were worth the money alone.

I had agreed to meet Caroline and the rest of the group at the Snowlands Restaurant later on that evening. When I got there, Walter told me that Caroline couldn't make it as she was feeling ill. I could understand why. The flight from China had brought her over three thousand metres in the space of a few hours. Sometimes, the body finds it difficult to cope with this rapid change in altitude. At three thousand seven hundred meters, Lhasa is one of the highest cities in the world and even walking along the streets can be a struggle if you are not properly acclimatised. I was disappointed that she couldn't join us. I had looked forward to spending more time with her.

The following day, I made the short bus journey from Lhasa to visit Nechung Monastery. During the reign of the Dali Lama, this was the seat of the State Oracle of Tibet. The Oracle was the medium through which the protector deity of Tibet spoke. The Tibetan government always consulted him before any impor-tant decisions were taken. The last State Oracle fled Tibet to India with the current Dalai Lama in 1959. The monastery was a strange place and unlike any other I'd seen so far. Just inside the entrance, there was a counter with bottles of Chinese rice wine for sale as offerings. In most monasteries, people buy butter to feed the lamps but, in this one, the rooms and chapels reeked of alcohol.

I entered the building and walked along the inner courtyard. The walls were decorated with shocking scenes of graphic vio-lence. Murals depicted flayed human skins hanging from rafters, people disembowelled by devils, dogs devouring the innards of the dead while others were impaled with spears. Im-ages of snakes slithering out of the eye sockets of skulls dotted the borders of many of the rooms. In one small chapel, a monk chanted a mantra in a deep, guttural tone while banging on a drum and crashing a cymbal. It had a very eerie effect and even the glass in the windows reverberated with the sound. It wasn't hard to imagine exorcisms and demonic possessions taking place there. This was not your usual Tibetan monastery.

I was reading Heinrich Harrer's book *Seven Years in Tibet*. He had written a stirring account of his time in Lhasa in the years before the Chinese invasion. His description of his visit to Nechung showed that the place had changed little.

"Hollow, eerie music greeted us at the gate of the temple. Inside, the spectacle was ghastly. From every wall looked down hideous, grimacing faces and the air was filled with stifling fumes of incense."

In his book, Harrer also gave an account of the rich ceremony that surrounded a meeting between Tibetan government offi-cials and the Oracle.

"[The Oracle] wore a round metal mirror on his breast. Attendants robed him in gay silks and led him to his throne. Then everyone drew back from around him. No sound could be heard except for the hollow music....He looked as if the life were fading out of him. Now he was perfectly motionless, his face a staring mask. Then suddenly, as if he had been struck by lightening, his body curved upward like a bow. The onlookers gasped. The god was in possession. The medium began to tremble; his whole body shook and beads of sweat stood out on his forehead. Servants went to him and placed a huge, fantastic head-dress on his head. This was so heavy that it took two men to carry it."

He also described how the government officials interacted with the Oracle.

"Servants held him fast and a Cabinet Minister came before him and threw a scarf over his head. He then began to ask questions carefully prepared by the Cabinet about the appointment of a governor, the discovery of a new Incarnation, matters involving war and peace."

After I had seen enough of the monastery, I left the building and walked along the dusty path behind it. Ahead of me, a herder struggled to keep his goats from straying. I passed mounds of rocks, topped with painted yak skulls. Huge images of the Buddha and Tsongkhapa, the founder of the Yellow Hat sect, were painted on the rock faces near the monastery. Nearby, men sat on the ground working on stones with hammers and chisels. They were carving special mani stones, religious slabs usually decorated with Sanskrit inscriptions or pictures of the Buddha. While some stones were unpainted, others were very colourful and made liberal use of bright yellows, blues, and reds. The workers chiselled away at the rock without taking their heads up, muttering prayers to themselves as they worked.

I left Nechung and returned to Lhasa. At the Yak Hotel, I

stopped by the travel office and browsed the notice board. One message there caught my eye. Two people were looking for others to share a jeep to the border with Nepal. They wanted to leave on the following Saturday and that suited my plans perfectly. The notice continued that anyone interested was to meet in the Snowlands Hotel at six that evening. I glanced at the clock and realised it was almost that time. I hurried there as fast as I could and bumbled into the Snowlands five minutes later. A few people looked at me as I stormed through the doors.

"Are you the people going to Nepal?" I asked breathlessly. A stocky man with long, black, unkempt hair stood up and approached me.

"Yes, we are. My name is Carlos."

Carlos introduced me to the others who had already agreed to travel south with him. My prospective travel partners were an international bunch. Carlos was Mexican and had assumed the role of group leader. His friend Geordie was an imposing but quiet Spaniard. Saskia was from Holland and whom I later realised was also staying at the Yak Hotel. Finally, he introduced the bookish and serious-looking Simon from Shanghai. Together, we agreed an itinerary to the border with Nepal, handed over our cash deposits to the travel company, and sorted out the final details of the trip. We were offered a choice between a road-hardened jeep and, for a little extra, a more comfortable Japanese Landcruiser. We opted for the Landcruiser and what a good choice it would turn out to be. We weren't able to meet our driver until the morning of the journey so we would have to wait until then to discover if he was an alcoholic or a madman.

My breath froze as I left the Yak Hotel to collect Caroline. It was just past six in the morning and was still dark. Early morning was supposed to be the best time to visit the Jokhang. The cold air made us shiver on the short walk to Barkhor Square, even with our heavy coats on. We were told that the doors of the temple would be opened at eight. There was an air of expectancy and excitement in the crowd, like a bunch of rock fans waiting for a glimpse of their idol or a crowd waiting for the last handful of cup final tickets to go on sale. People chanted, laughed, joked, and prayed as they waited. Most people had yellow or white silk scarves to give as gifts. Others held plastic containers of yak butter to feed the lamps. We bought a pair of scarves to present as gifts.

The guards finally appeared and the great doors of the temple swung open. The crush to get in was incredible and we allowed the crowd to push past us before entering the building ourselves. A queue had already formed for the main chapels but everyone was grinning with happiness and there were many friendly greetings exchanged. The pilgrims were from all across the Tibetan world, from the wild and warlike region of Kham in the east, from Amdo and Chamdo in the north, and from Shigatse in the south. There were nomads and businessmen, rich and poor, religious and otherwise.

The Jokhang consists of a number of small chapels off a main aisle, which leads to the main cathedral. We visited some of these tiny chapels, which were dedicated to various Buddhist deities and saints. Finally, we entered the main cathedral and saw the great statue of Buddha. The golden statue showed the Buddha at the age of twelve and is the most revered sculpture in Tibet. There was a terrific religious atmosphere around the statue. People prostrated in rows in front of the statue, monks chanted in unison, and temple custodians shuffled around filling the lamps with yak butter. The flickering lights of hundreds of lamps cast a pale glimmer around the otherwise darkened hall. People circled around the statue and then threw themselves full length on a plank of wood at its base. A huge monk stood behind the prostrating pilgrims and yanked them off the plank with one hand after a few seconds, thus keeping the line moving. I felt a bit of a fraud throwing myself on the plank and the monk didn't even have the decency to give me a good hard yank off it.

We decided to skip many of the smaller chapels and instead made a beeline for the roof. There, we were rewarded with a great view of the city with the Potala as a backdrop. We looked down on Barkhor Square as pilgrims prostrated in front of the temple. Fragrant smoke rose from a white chimney nearby and was scattered across the square by a light breeze. The Jokhang was a living place of worship and was exactly what the Potala had been missing. We left the magical Jokhang with chanting echoing in our ears.

I met up with Caroline and her friends later that night for supper. Walter, the Canadian, was leaving to continue his travels the next day. In typical Irish style, Caroline and I insisted in taking him out for a night on the town to wish him well on his journey. After a few beers, Walter decided to call it a night and returned to his hotel. Once Walter left, Caroline and I walked along the streets of Lhasa until we found a small restaurant with a big open fire near the Pentoc Hotel. We laughed and joked over a few drinks as we warmed ourselves in front of the roaring fire. I was enjoying my time with Caroline and wishing I didn't have to leave Lhasa so soon. I walked her back to her hostel and kissed her at the door of her guesthouse.

The next day was to be my last in Lhasa and I wanted to spend it with Caroline. We caught a bus to Sera Monastery, about five kilometres outside of Lhasa. After the incredible sights we had already seen, neither of us wanted to drag ourselves through chapel after chapel in another monastery. We were there for one thing and that was to see the debating monks.

At Sera, monks gather every day in the courtyard to debate Buddhist scripture. We found ourselves a nice spot in the courtyard and waited for the arrival of the monks. They filed in gradually and took up positions on the stony, tree-lined courtyard. Initially, they seemed to be very conscious of all the cameras and video recorders aimed in their direction. Once they started debating however, they got into the swing of things and totally forgot about us. Like the debating monks that I had seen in Labrang, the whole exercise was intended to help the students have a greater understanding of the scriptures they had learned. Some of the debaters seemed to be novices, while others were pure showmen with experience and swagger.

We felt we had enough of monasteries and caught a minibus back to Lhasa. We walked around Barkhor Square again hand in hand, listening to the people praying and enjoying the fragrant smell of juniper leaves burning. For me, this was what Lhasa was all about. Experiencing the religious devotion of hundreds of monks, nuns, and pilgrims was something very special. It gave the city an energy that I had never experienced in any other. I had wanted to believe that it would be like this, that there was still a place in the world like this. I was delighted to see that there was and it was alive and well. As we listened to the pilgrims chanting, Caroline leaned over to me and planted a kiss on my cheek.

"It would be nice to meet up again when we get home, wouldn't it?" she suggested with that smile, the smile I couldn't deny. I put my arm around her and squeezed her tight.

"It would," I admitted. "It would be very nice indeed." Four years later, I would marry her and make her my wife.

11

THE ROAD TO MOUNT EVEREST

Carlos was playing the fast dance tune 'Born Slippy' from the film *Trainspotting* when the Landcruiser rose over a crest on the road and we saw it for the first time. There was a collective gasp of amazement in four languages. Geordie switched the music off as we all stared ahead in wonder. It seemed too clear, too perfect, beyond anything I could have hoped for. Our driver stopped the vehicle and pointed to the highest peak in the serrated skyline.

"Everest," he said.

We had been on the road two days since leaving Lhasa, making overnight stops in the towns of Gyantse and Sakya in southern Tibet. During that time, we had crossed mountain passes over five thousand metres high, been treated to stunning views of sacred turquoise lakes, admired the gleaming crystal whiteness of vast glaciers, and visited ancient monasteries. During all that time, we had the lofty peaks and rugged countryside of Tibet for company. In itself, the journey from Lhasa was a

The awe-inspiring north face of Mount Everest

The Tibet Landcruiser gang, pictured before leaving Tibet

wonderful experience but for me, Everest and the Himalayas were the main attraction.

After our initial glimpse of the mountains, we drove on and an hour later, stopped at a high pass where the full glory of the Himalayas were revealed. Seeing the majestic giant of Mount Everest among its regal siblings is something I will never forget. Rugged, defiant, and rising high above all the others – it was exactly what the highest mountain in the world should look like. We all just stood there and gazed at the mountains, struck dumb by the wonder and majesty of nature.

The sight of the Himalayas promised to make the uncomfortable journey from Lhasa worthwhile. Between the five of us, the driver, and our mountains of baggage, there was little room to spare inside the Landcruiser. Since leaving Lhasa, we had agreed to take it in turns to sit in the back with the luggage. The Landcruiser didn't have a roof-rack and space was at a premium. We had started out from Lhasa on a sealed road but that had quickly deteriorated into a rutted and pot-holed trail. Already, our backsides were thanking us for having rented the Landcruiser as it was much more comfortable that the Jeep would have been. Our driver was a small but sturdy Tibetan named Stun-Sen, who had so far navigated the rough roads with great care and skill. Sten-Sen spoke little English but good Chinese so Simon sat up the front with him and they talked during most of the journey.

Before getting closer to the mountains, we had to stop for food. At the small settlement of Shegar, we dined on some overpriced noodles in a small restaurant. As we climbed back into the Landcruiser afterwards, local children dressed in filthy rags ran up to the windows with their hands outstretched. We tried to look away as they tapped the window and pleaded with us to give them some money or food. I felt ashamed to be travelling through their land in such relative luxury. We rolled down the window and handed out some biscuits and bananas to the children. That encounter in Shegar wasn't unique. The towns and villages along our route from Lhasa had looked impoverished. The driver returned and made the short journey to the government offices just outside the town. Qomolangma is what the Tibetans call Mount Everest and the Chinese government have designated the area around it to be a nature reserve, requiring all tourists entering it to purchase a permit. Once we'd done this, the driver left Shegar and took a left turn off the main road. For the next ninety kilometres, the Landcruiser bounced us about as the driver negotiated the rough route up the mountain. The road had plenty of sharp switchbacks and dangerous ravines that ensured our worried faces were kept plastered to the windows.

Geordie had turned out to be a technical wizard and had managed to hook up the Landcruiser's speakers to his iPod. Since then, music had accompanied us on the journey. The soft and soothing voice of Norah Jones had serenaded us as we left Lhasa, with the early morning mist rising out of the valley. The fast beat of Moby accompanied us as we sped across the open plains of southern Tibet. As we climbed the road towards Everest, Carlos had appointed himself DJ for the day and was treating us to his selection of his favourite tunes. He selected some great rock songs for the hairpin bends such as ACDC's *Thunderstruck* and Nirvana's *Smells Like Teen Spirit*. U2's *Beautiful Day* was belting out when we rounded a bend and saw the giant north face of Mount Everest filling the sky. If there was a more suitable soundtrack to that moment, I don't know it. It brought a lump to my throat, I won't lie.

We piled out of the Landcruiser at Rongphu, surely the highest monastery in the world. Trails of cloud were rising from the summit of Everest, like thin streams of steam blowing off the spout of a kettle. The imposing behemoth of The Mountain formed an impressive backdrop to the Tibetan stupa in front of the monastery. Simon wasted little time in setting up his tripod and camera in front of the stupa and making the most of the fading light.

We were staying at Rongphu Guesthouse, directly across from the monastery. I shared a draughty and basic room with Geordie. However, the view more than made up for any discomfort. The window in our room framed the north face of Everest which appeared to change colour with the setting sun, first turning a shade of orange and then red before disappearing into the darkness of the night. Even from the glassless window of the terrible squat toilet next door, the view would be worthy of a six-star hotel. As the sun disappeared, the temperature plummeted and I was reminded of how cold it could get in the mountains. Geordie's digital thermometer read minus fifteen degrees Celsius as we left the room to join the others in the kitchen.

Everyone was gathered around a small fire stove in the kitchen, rubbing their hands together furiously. I joined them and made some tea for myself. Despite the heat of the stove, it was so cold that nobody removed their hats or jackets.

As we warmed ourselves by the fire, I cast my mind back to a conversation I had with a man in a hotel bar in Lanzhou. I had only been passing through the city on my way to Xining. There wasn't anything to watch on the television in my hotel room so I went downstairs to the small bar. I ordered a beer and caught the gaze of another tourist sitting a few seats away. I introduced myself and we got talking. Harry seemed to be about fifty and spoke in a tough, American accent. He had deeply tanned skin and grey stubble covered his face. I told him about my plans to visit Tibet and see Mount Everest. The mention of The Mountain seemed to peak his interest.

"I suppose you've heard of Mallory and Irvine?" he asked. I nodded. They were two climbers who had attempted to climb Everest from the north face in 1924.

"Yes, many people have heard of them and their attempt to climb Everest. Some even believe that they may have reached the top before they died on the descent."

Harry took his gaze from his beer and looked directly at me.

"I think another man got there some time later, years before Hillary did. A man named Maurice Wilson." I confessed I had never heard of him.

"Maurice Wilson. A fascinating man, an incredible man," he gushed as he pulled his seat closer to me and readied himself for his story.

"Maurice Wilson was a man who believed that willpower could literally move mountains, or in his case, climb the highest one in the world. He was inspired after reading about the heroic but doomed attempt of Mallory and Irvine on Everest in 1924, and resolved to succeed where they had failed. For him, reaching the top of Everest became his life's quest."

Harry took a swig from his beer before continuing.

"Wilson was also a little eccentric, to say the least," he chuckled as he stroked his stubbled chin.

"His plan was to fly a plane to from England to India, crash land it on the upper slopes of Everest, before walking the rest of the way to the top." This was the plan of a lunatic, I thought. As it turned out, I was being kind to him.

"Wilson had no flying or mountaineering experience. The flight itself would have been a remarkable achievement for any aviator of the day, and a successful solo attempt to climb Everest had only been achieved as recently as 1980. His plan was wildly ambitious, to say the least."

"Excuse me," I interrupted. "Do you mean this man had no mountain experience, no alpine training?"

"Well, nothing that we would call mountain training," Harry replied. "Instead of learning how to use ice-picks, crampons, and climbing equipment, he walked the gentle hills of the Lake District in England and felt he was ready after two weeks. It took him twice as long as normal to get his pilot's license and his flight instructor begged him not to attempt his planned flight to India. Despite being forbidden from flying by the British Air Ministry, and only having two months flying experience, he departed from England in May 1933. All along his flight path to India, the British government obstructed him in every way possible. Despite all this, he landed in India two weeks later with his fuel-gauge reading zero. It was an incredible achievement."

Harry ordered two more beers and said nothing for the next few minutes, no doubt enjoying making me wait before continuing his tale.

"Once Wilson reached India, the British confiscated his plane so he had to make the rest of the way on foot. He reached Darjeeling, near the border of India and Tibet. Foreigners were not allowed into Tibet so he and two Sherpas disguised themselves as Buddhist monks, and walked across the mountains until they reached Rongphu Monastery. Leaving the Sherpas at the monastery, his first solo attempt at climbing Everest only lasted a week before he was forced to turn back to the monastery. Two weeks later, he tried again, this time with the Sherpas. They made it to about eight thousand metres before he left the Sherpas behind and continued towards the summit alone. He was never seen alive again."

I whistled in amazement. I had never heard of the man yet his achievements seemed unbelievable.

"After the Chinese climbed Everest in 1960, one of their group claims to have seen an old tent much higher than any British team had previously gone. I believe it may have been the tent of Maurice Wilson and that he may have reached the summit."

Harry anticipated my next question and cut across me.

"Of course, no one has any real proof of this but considering what the man did up to then, I don't think it's beyond the

121

realms of possibility that he made it."

Harry drained the last of his beer and pushed the empty bottle away.

"Your round," he smiled.

Sitting there around a fire stove in Rongphu, I began to understand the attraction of Everest. The Mountain drew Maurice Wilson towards it like a moth to a flame. The magnetism of the highest peak on Earth continues to draw people towards it to this day.

ꧦꧩꧦ

It wasn't destined to be my greatest night's sleep. Packs of dogs barked all night outside the window. I fell asleep for a while, but woke soon after to the incessant roaring of the bastards. I got some slight relief with thoughts of what I would do to them with baseball bat. It was so cold in the room that I wore my hat, trousers, jacket, and socks in bed but I was so restless during the night that I had to get rid of them all one by one. The base of the bed was made of what felt like old rickety wooden slats. Every time I shifted my weight, I felt sure the base would collapse, depositing me on the floor. I prayed hard for morning to come and an end to my thumping headache. I bruised my forehead from pressing my thumb against it to ease the pain. After what seemed like an eternity, light started to peek over the mountains. I could just make out the outline of Everest through the window. I heard people leaving their rooms and heading off on the nine kilometre walk to Everest Base Camp. I looked out the window and saw their thin beams of torch light wandering up the road and disappearing in the distance.

122

Like them, I had planned to walk to the base camp but after my lack of sleep, I didn't feel up to it that morning. I joined the others in the small kitchen where they were eating breakfast. When our driver offered to take us to Everest Base Camp, we all readily accepted. I ate some plain biscuits, washed down with a can of Red Bull in the hope that it might get me through the day. Once we were finished breakfast, we jumped into the Landcruiser and set off for Everest Base Camp.

The road to the base camp had been built by the Chinese to facilitate their attempt to climb Everest. I hadn't expected that we would be able to drive all the way there but was relieved when this proved to be the case. We arrived at base camp with Everest's north face looming larger than ever. Everest Base Camp didn't have much to it, just a concrete toilet and a small China Post kiosk that was closed until the summer. A sign indicated that we were at Qomolangma Base Camp, five thousand, two hundred, and twenty metres high. Boulders and rocks were scattered across the valley that led directly to The Mountain, as if some enormous trucks had dumped them there. Just beyond the sign, a metal plaque commemorated those who had died on Mount Everest. Most of the names inscribed seemed to be Russian. It was a reminder of the risks climbers faced when trying to conquer Everest and of the many bodies that lay unclaimed on the slopes of The Mountain.

We left Everest Base Camp behind and returned to the guesthouse to collect our bags. We then made our way downhill for our final night in Tibet in the town of Tingri. The driver said he could save time by taking a 'short-cut'. For the next few hours, we were thrown about violently as the Landcruiser negotiated boulders, rivers, ice, and nearly turned over on more than one occasion. We drove slowly down the face of steep embankments and zipped along roads that hugged steep cliffs. One mistake from the driver and we would have been plunged to almost certain death in the river below. The ease with which the driver handled the terrain showed how skilled he was. On the way down, we passed a heavily laden yak train. The beasts were tethered to each other and each carried numerous bags and containers. The animals had bells attached to them, which filled the air with a musical ringing as the caravan headed in the direction of the mountains. It was a wonderful sight from an ancient time.

ༀ

I suppose it's not fair to call Tingri a one horse town as there are in fact many horses here, many of them alive. We arrived in the town to find it was nothing but a glorified truck stop with some colour provided by the Tibetan nomads who stopped there for supplies. I was tired after the day, and felt listless and lethargic. The driver took us to Tingri Guesthouse and I agreed to share one of their cheapest rooms with Simon.

After supper, there was nothing left to do but go to bed. The light bulb in our room must have been the weakest ever made, and I felt I'd damage my eyes by trying to read in the semi-darkness. The night was destined to be another of barking dogs and restlessness. There's nothing worse than feeling exhausted but being unable to sleep. I listened to Simon's contented breathing as he slept and wished yet again for morning to come. I was ready to leave the Tibetan Plateau.

It was still dark when we piled into the Landcruiser the following morning one more time and drove slowly out of Tingri. Tibetan nomads were emerging from their tents just outside the town and I wondered how anyone could survive the deadly cold. I still felt exhausted from the lack of sleep and just lay back in the seat.

We hit our final high pass at five thousand metres with more astounding views of the Himalayas. I celebrated by getting sick at the side of the road. We had a short passport check at the small town of Nyalam before we started our dramatic descent off the Tibetan Plateau. The Landcruiser quickly descended a very steep road via a series of sharp switchbacks. We were plunged through clouds and into a completely new world. We drove through a truly spectacular valley with cascading waterfalls, rich vegetation, and houses perched on impossible cliff faces.

We finally arrived at the small but traffic-choked town of Zhangmu. Trucks and cars were backed up for miles on the Tibet side and it took us over two hours to get to the town centre. I immediately saw that we had arrived in a vastly different land. Dark skinned women wore colourful saris, and people babbled in a strange new language. Tibetans were still to be seen, if only in token numbers. This was not their land anymore. We said our goodbyes to Simon, who was returned to Lhasa with the Landcruiser. We thanked our driver Stun-Sen. He had been a safe and steady driver for us and in Tibet, that kind of driver is invaluable. We left them behind and passed through the Chinese border control. As we crossed the bridge that brought us into Nepal, I took one last look back at Tibet, but it was hidden from view, high beyond the clouds, in another world.

12

KATHMANDU

After crossing the border with Tibet, we wanted to get to Nepal's capital city of Kathmandu as quickly as possible. We had arrived in the small border town of Kodari and Kathmandu was about two hundred kilometres away. After making some inquiries, we were told that we had to first take a bus to the town of Barabise, and then take another one from there to Kathmandu. The alternative was to hire a faster but more expensive private jeep. We felt we could make it to Kathmandu before nightfall and we waited outside a small hotel for the bus to arrive. An hour later, Saskia lifted her head from her book and covered her mouth in shock at what she saw. I followed her gaze and cursed to myself. Groaning and creaking, the bus to Barabise rumbled down the road towards us. Its roof was crowded with people while others hung grimly from its sides. Through the cracked windscreen, I could see the wide-eyed driver gripping the wheel tightly as he struggled to keep the vehicle on the road. I resigned myself to getting an expensive jeep to Kathmandu instead of the bus. Surely, none of us would risk travelling on such a death trap. I hadn't reckoned on

Riding on the roof of the bus with Geordie

Meeting some local children in Kathmandu

Geordie.

As soon as the bus stopped, Geordie scrambled up the side ladder and onto the roof. I couldn't believe that he was actually thinking of taking the bus.

"Geordie, are you mad?" I shouted up at him.

"Come on up, it's great up here," he cried, with a slightly crazy look.

I looked at Saskia and Carlos and shrugged. We took a vote on whether or not to take the bus and I was soon clambering inside and forcing my way into a spare seat. The journey to Barabise would take four hours and the road was as rough and bumpy as anything I'd experienced in Tibet. My seat wasn't bolted to the floor so I went sailing across the aisle every time we took a sharp turn.

I struck up a conversation with a Nepali man who shared my moving seat. He was about thirty years old, thin but strong looking. He told me he had just returned to Nepal after working in Malaysia.

"It is very hard work there. The people there make me work very hard. We must go away to find work as it is very poor here in the countryside."

"Do a lot of people leave Nepal to look for work?" I asked.

"Yes, very many people. There is no work here for us. We have to leave to get work. Before, I worked for three years in Bahrain. The people treat me very bad there. Now, Malaysia is a little better."

Suddenly, the bus came to a halt. My neighbour looked out the window.

"Checkpoint," he muttered. "We must all get off the bus."

Khaki-clad soldiers boarded the bus and ordered us all off. We walked down the road a short distance to where we were to re-board the bus after it had been searched. Soldiers with rifles walked beside us as others manned heavy machine guns behind sandbag placements. The place bristled of weapons and fear.

This served as a vivid reminder of Nepal's ongoing civil war between the government and the Maoist rebels.

The Maoists had declared a war on the Nepali government in 1996 with the aim of ousting the King and replacing the government with a socialist one. The resulting conflict had so left over twelve thousand people dead. The Maoists were steadily growing in strength and had succeeded in blockading Kathmandu two months previously.

Once we got back on board, I asked my neighbour what the current situation was like.

"There is a curfew everywhere. No cars or people are allowed on the streets after eight thirty at night." He wasn't sure if this curfew applied to Kathmandu or not.

We reached Barabise only to learn that the last bus to Kathmandu had already departed and we would have to stay the night. I was dejected. Ever since Lhasa, I had been looking forward to enjoying the simple pleasures of a hot shower, a comfortable bed, and a few cold beers in Kathmandu. That would have to wait for one more night as Barabise wasn't really set up for tourists. We chose to stay in the aptly named Ratti Hotel which, to be fair, turned out to be just fine. It had lukewarm showers and lumpy beds but, after my nights in Rongphu and Tingri, it might as well have been the Ritz.

As we tucked into a meal in the hotel restaurant, we could hear the shutters crashing down on shops across the town in preparation for the curfew. The lights on the street outside flickered off one by one until the little town was plunged into total darkness. After supper, I went back to the room to read for a while. The river outside the window gurgled gently as I lay on the bed and tried to read. It wasn't long before my heavy eyes closed and I drifted off into a deep and luxurious sleep. It felt good to be in the lowlands again.

I woke the next morning feeling refreshed for the first time in a week. It felt good to be able to sleep soundly again. After a light breakfast, we bought our tickets to Kathmandu and boarded a similar bus to the one from the day before. Once again, Geordie climbed up onto the roof, grinning like a kid. We passed our bags up to him and he secured them. Once I passed my rucksack to him, I climbed up and joined him. We tried unsuccessfully to get Saskia and Carlos to join us on the roof. I was about to see what rooftop riding was all about.

We shared the roof with a few locals who were transporting churns of milk. This really was the best seat on the bus. As the wind rushed through my hair, I took in Nepal's spectacular scenery. Mountains soared to the heavens, their heads hidden in distant clouds. People worked and toiled in rice paddies far below us. Lush and wooded valleys plunged off the sides of the mountains to join the thundering waters of the mighty Bhote Khosi River far below us as it flowed off the Tibetan Plateau.

After a while, I lay back on my rucksack with my hands locked behind my head. The sun shone brightly in a cloudless sky and warmed my face. I closed my eyes and thought of what I might would be doing at home if I hadn't decided to take this trip. There were times when I questioned the wisdom of making such a journey. Should I be looking for a job instead of wandering around Asia? Should I be saving to buy a house instead of spending money on guidebooks and backpacks? All those questions were answered on the roof of that bus and I thanked God that I had made the decision to travel. It was sobering to imagine myself behind an office desk at home, banging away at a computer, attending mind-numbing meetings, and wishing away each hour of the day. Instead, I was on my way to the magical city of Kathmandu on the roof of a bus, surrounded by majestic mountains. It was a lovely moment.

A few miles outside Kathmandu, our time on the roof ended as the conductor asked us all to come inside the bus. We endured one final checkpoint before we arrived in Kathmandu. After we left the bus, we collected our bags and delved into the heart of the city. Soon, we found ourselves in a warren of narrow streets with tall buildings on both sides. Rickshaws, taxis, and motorbikes all battled for a passage through the narrow lanes. We decided to stay at a place called Garden House in the tourist area of Thamel. It would be our base while in Kathmandu

Once I'd unpacked, it was time to check my e-mail, which I hadn't done in over a week. I was very relieved to find that there were no urgent messages waiting for me. E-mail was the only way for friends and family to get in touch with me while I was travelling. I got a message from my old college friend Eoin 'Butch' Canny, who informed me that he was on his way to Kathmandu from India. This was great news as I was really looking forward to seeing a familiar face.

After relaxing in the guesthouse for a while, we wandered down Thamel's main street. Despite the on-going civil war, there were plenty of tourists about in the city. Thamel was crammed with businesses dedicated to the needs of visiting tourists. Hotels and guesthouses were cheap and plentiful while travel shops offered hiking tours to Sikkim and the Annapurnas, as well as white-water rafting and bungee jumping. Good restaurants served Thai, Indian, European, and even Nepali dishes. After the desolate emptiness of Tibet, it would take a while to get used to all of this.

After our journey from Lhasa, we had all been looking forward to a good night out. We found just the place for it in a bar called Full Moon, just off the main street in Thamel. Carlos and Saskia danced to the music while Geordie and I keep the beers coming. I got chatting to an Englishman named Peter who was living in Kathmandu and married to a Nepali girl. He was a good source of information on Nepal's seedier current affairs. He told me that in 2001, the Nepali royal family had been massacred by the crown prince, who had then killed himself. This made the king's brother Gyanendra the ruling monarch. Peter firmly believed that Gyanendra had a hand in the massacre. He also believed that the Maoists would eventually win the war, as the government seemed to be totally impotent and corrupt. The beer flowed and the party continued late into the night.

The next morning, I was woken by a knock on my room door and I opened it to the beaming face of my good friend Butch. He had found me from the address I had e-mailed him. It was great to see a familiar face. After I freshened up, we went off to have breakfast at the swanky Kathmandu Guesthouse where Butch was staying. There, I met Jolien and Loneke, the two Dutch girls he was travelling with. There was a buffet breakfast on offer and I attacked it with glee. I piled my plate high with scrambled eggs, toast, sausages, and potatoes. This was accompanied by a cup of freshly ground coffee and fresh orange juice. I ate with the abandon and urgency of a person who had lived off noodles for far too long. Both hands worked furiously to cram food into my mouth. After a while, even my emergency belt notch couldn't handle the pressure of my expanding stomach. After I finished, I slumped into my chair like a boxer after twelve rounds and allowed my stomach digest the luscious food.

After I recovered from the breakfast buffet, Butch and I set off to explore Kathmandu. We made a beeline for Durbar Square, one of the city's main attractions. Magnificent shrines and ancient temples surround the square. We began a whirlwind tour of temples and Gods, from Shiva to Ganesh, from Hindu deities to Buddhist stupas. As we examined one wooden temple, Butch grabbed me by the shoulder and pointed up at the carvings on the wooden struts.

"Take a look at this," he cried, full of excitement.

Some wildly erotic scenes were carved all over the wooden

struts. The carvings were crude but to the point. The scenes depicted couples engaged in athletic sex in a wide range of positions, a woman copulating with a horse, and a number of threesomes. We gazed up at the various arches for ages, fascinated but unsure why these carvings should appear on a Nepali temple. I was later told that the Goddess of Lightening is a virgin, who wouldn't dare strike a building decorated with such carvings. It's a nice story, whatever the truth. A line of soldiers marched by as we were admiring the carvings. Apart from ourselves, no one seemed to notice them. Soldiers and guns seemed to be part of daily life in Kathmandu.

We were both tired after our respective journeys from Tibet and India, so we just ambled around the temples listlessly. We sat on the top steps of the 'Hippie Pagoda', a popular hangout for travellers in the sixties. Butch had arrived in India a few weeks earlier but had already covered an impressive amount of ground. We talked about our travels so far while fending off the touts that worked the popular square. A woman from a local television station called Channel Nepal was interviewing people on the pagoda. She approached us and asked us a few questions in English for her music video show. She signalled to the cameraman and he started recording. The lovely interviewer asked us what we were doing in Nepal. Before Butch could answer, I told her that we were touring Nepal with our new band 'Los Grandes Calientes Cojones' (Spanish for big hot balls). Carlos and Geordie had dreamed up this fictional band during the long drive from Lhasa. It was the band they hoped to form if they ever won the lottery. Now, it had the chance to live. I steadied myself and told her that the band played an eclectic mix of classical, rock, and trash metal. I stared into the camera and barked at the viewing public to go and buy our number one hit, 'Saskia'. Butch had a very hard time keeping a straight face.

After seeing Durbar Square, Butch returned to his guesthouse and I went to buy a few things in Thamel. On the way there, I bumped into Geordie, who raved to me about an amazing shave he had just received from a neighbourhood barber. He was so impressed that he insisted on showing me the place immediately. He led me through narrow lanes until we came to a small blue doorway. I peered inside and saw the barber at work, giving an old man a haircut. His little shop seemed tired and tattered. The mirrors were cracked and the only two seats available were patched up with insulating tape. The barber himself wore a white coat with buttons done up to his neck. I glanced back at Geordie nervously. The last thing I wanted was to get an infection from a dirty shaving blade. Geordie ushered me inside just as the old man left. The barber spoke no English but Geordie stood beside me, stroking his smooth face and the barber understood. He showed me to a seat and first applied some hot towels to my face for a few minutes. Once he removed the towels, he then lathered thick shaving foam on my face. I swallowed hard when the barber started to sharpen the cut-throat razor, moving the gleaming razor up and down on a leather belt with rhythmic motions. Carefully, he ran the razor over my face like the well-practiced master that he was. Once my shave was complete, he towelled my face off and re-applied the shaving foam a second time. Once more, he ran the razor over my face with slow and skilful motions. Once the shave was complete, he massaged my face, head, neck, and shoulders before finally applying a cooling lotion to my skin. For the remainder of that day, I couldn't help stroking my face and marvelling at how smooth it was. To this day, it is still the best shave I've ever had.

On my way back to the guesthouse, I ran into a bunch of kids who were just leaving school. They greeted me with a chorus of "Hellos" before starting a barrage of playful questions such as where I from was, how did I like Nepal, and how old I was. In return, I lined them up in return and asked them some questions. They were great fun as they talked about their boy-friends, girlfriends, rap music, and hip-hop. Most of them were only about ten years old. When I tried to leave, some of them latched onto my arms and legs and made me promise to visit their school before I left Kathmandu. Laughing, I promised I would.

At breakfast the following morning, I asked Butch about his travel plans after Kathmandu. There was only one thing on his mind.

"Into the mountains Johnny, into the Annapurnas," he said. I had hoped he would say that as I was planning to go there my-self. The Annapurna Mountains were part of the Himalayas and offered some of the best hiking in Nepal. We agreed to go there together and I was thrilled to have Butch and the Dutch girls along for the journey.

Before leaving for the Annapurnas, I had to sort out my visa to India, the next leg of my journey. If the process were any-thing like the one at the Nepal-Tibet border, then it would be a pleasure. There, the Nepali visa office was a sparse concrete building with simple wooden furniture. It was staffed by a sour looking man, seated behind a worn-looking desk. We filled out a visa form, paid ten American dollars, and we had our visa. Obtaining a visa to India would not prove so straightforward.

I strolled over to the Indian embassy building after my breakfast and I was a bit surprised to see a long queue of people waiting to get in. This had me a bit worried. As I got closer to the tourist visa section, I could see people at the counter arguing heatedly with embassy officials. After a two hour wait, a bu-reaucrat beckoned me to approach the counter.

"I'd like to apply for a visa please," I said with total inno-cence.

"Give me embassy clearance form," he moaned, with barely concealed distain.

"Embassy clearance, what's that?" I replied.

He threw his head back in a fit of laughter and shouted something to one of his friends behind him, who just shook his head. To my horror, he explained to me that the visa process was not a simple one. First, a visa applicant must get an embassy clearance form, complete it, and submit it. The embassy clearance alone would take about a week to come through. Only then was it possible to apply for the actual visa, which would take a number of days longer. I grabbed a clearance form and walked back to the guesthouse. I had seriously underestimated the amount of time it would take to get an Indian visa in Nepal. I decided to visit the embassy early the following day, get my clearance form submitted, and meet Butch in the Annapurnas. That way, I hoped to do some trekking in the mountains while my embassy clearance was being sorted out.

That evening would be the last that I would spend with the gang from the Tibet Landcruiser. Saskia, Carlos, and Geordie were all going their separate ways the following day. We met for a lovely meal and laughingly recounted the long journey that had taken us from Lhasa to Kathmandu. I hoped to keep in touch with them all after the journey had ended. I returned to the guesthouse early to pack for the mountains.

Before I left Kathmandu the following morning, I stopped at the children's school as promised. I knocked on the door and awkwardly asked the teacher permission to talk to the class. She agreed and welcomed me in. I looked around and recognised some of the kids from the day before. They were giddy with excitement and looked genuinely happy to see me. Their teacher then asked the children to come forward. The ones I had spoken to the previous day filed towards me one by one. They each handed me a card they had made. One or two of them threw their arms around my waist after giving me the card. One of the cards had the words 'Happy Christmas' written on it, and a painting of a figure that I assumed was Santa Claus. Another had a pencil drawing of someone crying huge tears and the words 'I will miss you' written below. Even though I had only known them for fifteen minutes, meeting the children that day in the classroom was the best memory I have of Kathmandu. Even when the memory of the temples of Durbar Square has long faded, I will still remember those children, with their honest curiosity and simple affection.

After I returned to the guesthouse to finish packing, I looked through the children's cards once again. One card in particular caught my attention. It was a crayon drawing of some perilously high looking mountains. A dangerous looking animal with sharp teeth and claws was crouched behind a rock, as if waiting for some unsuspecting victim to appear. Nearby, a white-faced figure with huge glasses walked unsuspectingly towards the trap. Under the drawing appeared the words, 'Please be careful in the mountains'. The Annapurnas had just become a much more frightening place to me.

PostScript:

In response to a wave of pro-democracy protests in Nepal in 2006, King Gyanendra reinstated parliament that he had previously dissolved. Once reinstated, parliament moved quickly to reduce the powers of the King. In December 2007, a bill was passed which effectively removed the King as Head of State, thereby ending the monarchy and declaring Nepal a federal republic.

13

THE CATHEDRALS OF ICE

"Sir, sir, come with me. I will give you a very good room," one boy shouted at me as I got off the bus in Pokhara.

"No sir, he has bad rooms. I will show you much better rooms," cried another as he tried to pull my rucksack off my shoulders. People crowded around me and shouted offers of accommodation at me from all directions. There was an air of desperation in their voices that was a bit frightening. With people pulling and pleading, I didn't know which way to turn.

In the midst of the mayhem, I spotted a man holding up a cardboard sign with my name on it. Butch had mentioned that he would try to have someone meet me off the bus and I was delighted that he remembered. When I told the mob that I already had accommodation, they trooped off dejectedly.

The taxi dropped me at the Rustik Guesthouse where Butch, Jolien, and Loneke were staying. As soon as I'd booked in, Butch marched me to the hiking permit office. All hikers are required to purchase a permit before heading off into the mountains. We had decided to walk the eight-day Annapurna Sanctuary Trek, which would take us into the heart of the

Hein, Butch, Jolien, and Loneke

The majestic peak of Machhapuchhre

Himalayas. At the office, I handed over two thousand rupees to a dubious looking official for a permit that I suspected I'd never need. Once that was taken care of, we collected Jolien and Loneke, and walked the short distance into town to get some food.

Nature has been kind on Pokhara. The shores of the lovely Lake Phewa lap against one side of the town while the majestic Annapurnas form an impressive backdrop on the other. It's a perfect base for hikers and climbers destined for the Himalayas. Located in central Nepal, Pokhara is about a five-hour bus journey from Kathmandu. As we walked along the main street, we watched the army stop and search some random people. Other soldiers kept a nervous watch as they cradled machine guns in their arms. This was part of everyday life in Pokhara. It was hard to believe that, only miles from this beautiful setting, a civil war was going on. Many shop owners would lament how the number of visitors to Pokhara had fallen due to the conflict. For a town so dependant on tourist income, such a drop was deeply felt. I could understand the desperation of the young touts at the bus station that morning.

Despite the drop in tourists, Pokhara was still open for business. The main street was dotted with signs advertising pizzas, steaks, burgers, and chips. Inside many bars, young backpackers swilled bottles of Heineken as they cheered on their football team on the big screen, beamed directly from Europe. Shops selling bootleg CDs and DVDs blasted the latest music hits from Europe and America. Clothing stores advertised the big hiking brands such as North Face and Colombia. However, so many of these branded items were imitations that people had jokingly started calling them North Fake or North Farce. We found a restaurant that Butch had heard about, and we were soon enjoying a delicious pizza while watching the film *As Good As It Gets* on a big screen. I talked with Jolien and Loneke for a while. They had both taken a year out to travel after finishing University in Holland. They were both very fun loving and were great to be around. With such good food and entertainment, it was easy to forget that we were in rural Nepal. It was a very pleasant way to end my first day in Pokhara.

I rolled out of bed early the next morning and joined Loneke and Jolien on the rooftop restaurant for breakfast. I was glad I did. We were treated to some superb views of the Annapurnas as the morning sun bathed them in light. The main peak is called Machhapuchhare – also known as The Fishtail due to its distinctive shape – and it stood out from the rest as the jewel in the crown. It was a true Himalayan peak, a Matterhorn of the Himalayas. It was considered so sacred that climbers were forbidden from trying to scale it. It was a pure, unconquered colossus and I couldn't wait to get closer.

As I packed for the trek, I tried to bring only the bare essentials as I intended to leave most of my belongings at the guesthouse. The guesthouse manager soon appeared to inform us that our taxi had arrived to take us to the start of the trail. We went outside to see a rusting Datsun waiting for us. I didn't think there would be enough room in the small car but somehow, we managed to squeeze our bags, gear, and ourselves inside it. Hiking boots were crammed under seats and jackets stuffed into every available space. Once we were all in, the car coughed and spluttered before the driver managed to coax the engine into starting. With a smile of relief, he drove onto the main road at speed, narrowly missing an oncoming truck. So began our journey into the mountains.

It was a long, winding and narrow road that seemed to snake forever upwards into the Himalayan foothills. I was sitting in the passenger seat when I heard a strange noise coming from the direction of the cassette player. The driver noticed my interest.

"You like Nepali music?" he asked, incredulously.

"Sure," I replied politely.

"Then you will like this Nepali rock music for sure."

He turned the volume up to the maximum as the speakers emitted a screeching sound that assaulted my ears. It was hard to decide whether to blame the poor quality of the cassette player or the band's lack of talent. I looked back helplessly at the gang crushed in the back seat and mouthed "sorry."

For most of the journey, we were stuck behind a smoke-belching lorry, which we were unable to pass. For hours, I stared ahead at the back of that lorry while trying to block out the driver's ear-busting music. Eventually, we reached the small town of Nayapul, where the hiking trail into the mountains begins. We paid the driver and resisted his pleadings for more money because of our extra bags. I told him that I enjoyed the Nepali rock music and to look for a band called *Los Grandes Calientes Cohunes*, the fictional band that we had invented in Tibet. I even wrote it down for him in case he forgot. He clutched the note and thanked me. That'll keep him busy some weekend, I thought. As he sped off, we turned and started to walk, something that we'd be doing almost continuously for the next eight days.

༄༅༎

After sitting on buses and trains for the last few weeks, it felt good to get some exercise. With our backpacks on, we laughed and joked as we walked towards the mountains. We passed people working in paddy fields and others tending vegetables in their small plots of land. The sun shone brightly and we were soon sweating heavily under our backpacks. Despite having left most of my stuff in Pokhara, my bag felt heavy. One by one, the jackets and layers came off until I was soon down to my t-shirt.

As our pace slowed, we were overtaken by local people

carrying huge loads in long wicker baskets. They were followed closely by mules, laden down with goods. Children followed the mules carrying goods in cloth bags on their backs. For the many lodges and villages deep in the heart of the mountains, this was the only way to get supplies. Not long afterwards, a man jogged by us with a huge black plastic water tank on his back. As he disappeared around the bend, he looked like an ant carrying a huge piece of food.

The path was well maintained, with stone steps lining the route almost continuously. We passed through some small villages that sold a wide range of goods for trekkers including chocolate, beer, rum, and soft drinks. Locals and trekkers alike greeted us with a friendly wave and "Namaste" (Nepali for Hello) as we walked.

At the start of the trail, we had set a brisk pace and had found the going easy. However, as the grade got steeper, we were breathing hard and just concentrating silently on the track ahead. I was getting tired as we trod endlessly upwards towards the mountains. Butch and Jolien both were fit and had little difficultly with the steep path. Loneke walked with me for most of the day, both of us concentrating silently on the path ahead. At the higher reaches of the mountains, farmers had worked the sheer slopes into terraces for rice and vegetables. The terraces continued in steps down into the valley floor far below. Without this system, agriculture would be impossible on such steep mountain slopes. People were clinging to the sides of the Himalayas like limpets to rocks.

As darkness started to fall, we arrived at the village of Gandruk, where we had planned to finish our first day's trek. We walked to the end of the village and booked ourselves into a place called Excellent View Guesthouse. It was cosy and homely with bright flowers in the front garden as well as wicker chairs to relax in. Beehives hung from the eves of the roof so we stayed well away from that area. The proprietor put on a roaring fire in the front yard and we all sat around it and ordered beers and pizza. Ah, the rigours of travel! The quality of the food was excellent considering what a small and rural village Gandruk was. This would prove to be typical along the trail as each guesthouse provided high quality food. It was lovely to warm ourselves in front of a fire with good food and beer, watching the light fade on the lofty Himalayan peaks. It was a fitting end to a great day.

As we enjoyed our meal, we were joined by a Belgian trekker, who was also staying at the guesthouse. Hein was a man who had reached the end of his patience with travel. He unloaded a litany of bad luck stories on us. He had been robbed in India, missed his flight to Nepal, encountered rude and corrupt airport officials, and had a generally miserable time while in Asia.

"I have always wanted to travel on my own," he explained. "I have a wife and three kids back in Belgium and I wanted to see if I could be on my own. I have not been on my own for over twenty five years." He stared into the fire mournfully. "It does not seem that I can manage on my own."

Hein intended to abandon his trek the next day and return to Pokhara. We tried to encourage him and asked him to join us in hiking to Annapurna Base Camp. We argued that, after what he had gone through, he might as well go the last stretch with us. He didn't seem convinced but promised to think about it and let us know the following morning. As the fire slowly died out and robbed us of its warmth, we realised how cold it was and we were soon making for our beds. It was only 9 P.M. but it would turn out to be one of the latest nights we'd have on the trek.

Hein joined us at breakfast the following morning and announced that he had changed his mind and would join us on our trek. We were delighted as he was a nice guy who has just suffered a run of bad luck. I wasn't in the mood for breakfast as

145

I didn't feel well that morning. Walking was the last thing I wanted to do but I decided to push on anyway as I didn't want to hold the group back. It would turn out to be the hardest day I had put down in a long time.

We started the day by descending a long line of stone steps towards the river. I was happy that we didn't have to climb any steep paths. However, in this part of the world, a steeper walk uphill always follows a downhill. Even on this easy grade, I felt weak and had to stop every hundred meters for a break. We reached the bottom of the valley and crossed a wooden bridge to a small guesthouse. I collapsed exhausted into a seat and tried unsuccessfully to eat a bowl of instant noodles.

I asked the owner of the guesthouse about the path ahead. I'll never forget his answer.

"Yes, the route is flat," he assured me. Relief washed over me. He then seemed to remember himself.

"Nepali flat, not Western flat," he added ominously.

A Nepali would probably consider a forty-five degree incline flat. God only knows what he would have thought of as steep. I grimaced at his reply and steeled myself for what lay ahead.

We had only gone a short while from the guesthouse when the trail rose up a steep and bleak looking hill. It was a hill that I will forever remember as *El Bastardo*. The trail never stopped going upwards, always upwards. It continued climbing along stone steps, across rough paths, and through ploughed fields. It never seemed to end. Every time I thought we had reached the top, it would climb higher still. Sweat poured freely from my body as I cursed and swore loudly. My stomach churned and my head throbbed.

Hein proved to be very fit and found the steep path little trouble. He spoke Dutch so he was able to converse easily with Loneke and Jolien. He seemed to be enjoying the company.

I was slowing the group down a lot by my increasingly frequent breaks for water and rest. I spent most of the day with my hands on my knees, gasping for air and feeling like throwing up. Despite the delays I was causing, nobody complained. However, I was conscious of it myself and that made me even grumpier than before. The following scene played itself out a number of times during my frequent stops for water.

"What would he do?" I asked aloud, the question aimed at no one in particular.

"What would who do?" Butch asked, probably worrying about my sanity.

"Chris Bonington, what would he do in my situation?"

Chris Bonington was the legendry mountaineer who had led the first successful expedition to scale the notorious south face of Annapurna in 1970.

Before Butch had time to answer and suggest that I should take a few tablets, I continued my rant.

"Would Chris Bonington give up? Would he say, 'I've had enough?' No."

At that point, I would make a big scene of standing up and hauling my bag on my back like a war hero carrying his wounded friend from the field of battle.

"Chris Bonington would carry on and so will I," I would roar and with that, I would start up the path once more, talking to myself, and cursing loudly when I missed a step. What must the rest of the group have thought?

Whatever malady affected me, it had robbed my energy. I felt mentally and physically exhausted and only brute stubbornness kept me going. Butch showed what a good friend he was and kept encouraging me on by saying we were nearly at the top of the hill. Poor Butch would then have to take the stream of abuse as the path ascended higher still.

Finally, mercifully, we reached the top of the hill. I was too exhausted to be happy. It was downhill from there to the village of Chhomrong. We reached it eight hellish hours after leaving Gandruk. I slumped to the ground outside a guesthouse called

Himalayan View and could go no further. The landlady promised me a good hot shower and God bless her, did she deliver. To call standing under the life-giving streams of hot water orgasmic would only be to hint at the joy I felt. I laughed aloud as the water danced off my skin and seemed to restore my energy. Butch gave me some American headache pills and I went for a rest. When I joined everyone for supper that evening, my appetite had returned and I was feeling a lot better.

I woke the next morning feeling refreshed and ready for the day ahead. I tucked into a breakfast of oatmeal with apples and honey, washed down with lemon tea. I would enjoy that breakfast combination many times over the next few days. We had a long day's walk ahead but I felt strong. As we left Chhomrong, we passed a sign advertising the last hot showers on the trail. There was a very steep path on the opposite side of the river but I got into a steady walking rhythm, matching my breathing to my steps. After a while, I was in a semi-hypnotised state as I counted out the steps to myself. At one point, I had to make way for a man who was walking briskly up the steep path with an entire chicken coup on his back, complete with chickens. The chickens looked calm enough, everything considered. Loneke was struggling a bit and had to stop frequently for a rest. It seemed that it was her turn to feel the strain.

In the areas beyond Chhomrong, I saw many signs in support of the Maoists. One sign said 'Long Live People's Liberation Army of Nepal. Long live the Great People's War. CPN (Maoist).' It was in these mountains, far from the government in Kathmandu, that the Maoists had their base. People living in rural areas of Nepal feel that the government has abandoned them. There were no jobs or prospects for these poor and desperate people. Officials were corrupt and had no interest in the welfare of the local population. It is a story that is repeated the world over. A desperate and deprived people, neglected by a corrupt government, become easy prey for an

148

extreme group promising change, jobs, and respect. The Maoists filled that role in Nepal.

We soon entered a very pleasant wooded area of Rhododendron trees that reminded me of Ireland. The trees provided shade from the sun and made it perfect for walking. Now and again, snow-capped peaks peered through the leafy branches of the trees. We sensed that we were getting closer to the mountains. We stopped at the settlement of Bamboo for lunch. It's a place known for its weed but we weren't offered any. However, we were offered the last hot showers on the trail, this time for real. We had hoped to get as far as the settlement of Dovan that day and by late afternoon, we had reached it with little trouble. We considered continuing on to the next settlement of Himalaya Hotel. Loneke was really struggling at that stage and it was up to her if she wanted to continue. To her eternal credit, she showed real determination and pushed on. Butch again showed what a gentleman he was by carrying her bag for her the rest of the way.

At one point, we crossed a long metal suspension bridge that spanned a roaring river. A plaque informed us that the Gurkhas had erected the bridge for the benefit of the local people. The Gurkhas are the Nepali branch of the British Army and had erected or paid for several bridges in the area. For many people in rural Nepal, joining the Gurkhas offered a way to escape poverty.

The route to Himalaya Hotel was a lot longer that we had estimated and it was nearly dark when we got there. The place was not a hotel at all but two guesthouses next to each other. Loneke was too exhausted to eat and went straight to bed. The rest of us joined some other hikers in the kitchen for some food. I asked if anyone had encountered the Maoists along the way. An Australian told me about the Maoist taxation system. In many parts of the Annapurnas, he said, the Maoists collect a tourist 'tax' from the hikers they encounter. Apparently, the process is conducted in a very mannerly fashion. The Maoists enter the lodge where hikers are staying and politely request a voluntary donation to the Maoist cause. As the 'donations' are collected, the local Maoist leader gives a talk about how the money will be used for local hospitals and how the government are hurting the people. In one lodge, an Israeli had apparently tried to resist the tax but a gun pointed at his head convinced him to comply. After the money is handed over, everyone is given an official receipt so that the person is not charged twice in another village. Luckily, we never encountered the Maoists or their tax requests along the route.

As had happened to me, Loneke awoke the next morning feeling better and ready for the day ahead. That day, we planned to walk the short but steep distance to Machhapuch-hare Base Camp. We got some nice views of the Annapurnas before we set off from the lodge. For most of the morning, the sun remained hidden behind the lofty peaks that surrounded us. It was almost 10 A.M. before the valley was finally flooded with sunlight and warmth. The scenery started to look alpine and more like the Himalayas that I had expected. Snow and ice covered both sides of the track as we climbed higher.

Soon, the valley narrowed until it became a canyon between the mountains of Machhapuchhre and Hiunchuli. It was the doorway to one of the most beautiful places on Earth. We emerged into a vast, mountain-ringed amphitheatre that was the Annapurna Sanctuary. We were surrounded by some of the highest mountains in the world including Annapurna, Gangapurna, and Machhapuchhre. I found that I could hardly go ten metres without stopping to gaze open-mouthed at those spectacular mountains. Their awesome beauty humbled me. It was as if I had entered a place that was not part of the world. The hand of man was not visible here, and there were no permanent settlements to be seen. That place is too high for people to live. Only the Gods dwell there.

150

Tired but happy, we reached Machhapuchhare Base Camp via a long series of wearying stone steps. We were within sight of Annapurna Base Camp but decided to stay put for the night in order to acclimatise.

Jolien and Loneke took advantage of the break to write some notes so that they could update their web blog when they got back to Pokhara. Hein just relaxed and read some books. I whiled away the evening by teaching Butch how to play chess and then going off in a huff when he beat me in his first game. He came out to where I was sulking on the deck of the guest-house and produced a hip flask.

"For emergencies," he smiled, offering me the flask. I swigged down good Black Bush whiskey and all was right with the world again. The girls and Hein joined us on the deck and we watched the sun go down on Machhapuchhare. Watching it change colour in the fading light, I can understand why it is considered sacred. The Sanctuary had a very spiritual and sacred feeling about it.

Everyone was in good spirits the next morning as we made our way upwards towards Annapurna Base Camp. Watching the sun peek over Machhapuchhare before finally emerging and washing the valley in light, is a sight that I will never forget. We reached our goal of Annapurna Base Camp at ten that morning and congratulated ourselves on our achievement. I celebrated with a plate of fried potatoes at the small lodge.

The mountains limited the time the sun was actually visible, so by two that afternoon the light had started to fade. Butch and I spent the afternoon scrambling up an ice-covered hill behind the lodge. It was a lot trickier that I had anticipated and I was glad to get down off it safely. I decided to name it The Butch Step in honour of our expedition leader.

Butch and I wandered up to the ridge above the lodge to watch the sunset. The area was dotted with prayer flags and cairns of stones, some of them with inscriptions about people who had died on the Annapurnas. Like Everest, the Annapurnas had claimed its share of climbers, exacting a high price for the chance to conquer these mountains. One monument was to the Russian climber Anatoli Boukreev, who died climbing Annapurna in 1997. His body was never recovered. I knew of his name from the book *Into Thin Air*, which seemed to partially blame him for the disastrous expedition to Everest in 1996.

Hein joined us on the ridge a while later.

"It's bloody cold up here," he exclaimed as he stuffed his hands deeper into his down jacket. Butch took the hint and passed him the hip flask. He swigged from it and passed it back to Butch.

"Thanks" he said. "Thanks for inviting me along with you guys. I'm really happy to have made it up here and to have met such good people." The feeling was very mutual.

"This place is really something else," he admitted as he scanned the ring of mountains. "Really something else."

We watched the mountains change with the setting sun. A bank of clouds floated below the snow-covered peak of Machhapuchhare until it appeared to be disembodied, floating in the sky. The hidden sun reflected its light off the clouds, splashing them with marvellous hues of pink, red, and orange. On the opposite side of the valley, the colossus of Hiunchuli was also undergoing some remarkable changes. The top half of the mountain started to glow with a golden colour until it looked like the snow was on fire. We watched this unfold in silence, in awe. We stayed up on the ridge as long as we could bare it. Soon, the full moon lit the valley with a dull glow and the place suddenly seemed unearthly, as if we were standing on some distant Martian world. Our journey into the mountains had ended. The next day, we would start back down towards Pokhara again. We'd soon be surrounded by bars offering pizzas, movies, and live English football. Within a few days, I'd have to part ways with Butch, Jolien, Loneke and Hein to continue my journey to India. It was hard to disagree with the words of Boukreev that were inscribed on a plaque.

"Mountains are not Stadiums where I satisfy my ambition to achieve, they are the cathedrals where I practice my religion...I go to them as humans go to worship. From their lofty summits I view my past, dream of the future and, with an unusual acuity, am allowed to experience the present moment...my vision cleared, my strength renewed. In the mountains I celebrate creation. On each journey I am reborn."

14

CITY OF DEATH

"Benares [Varanasi] is older than history, older than tradition, older even than legend, and looks twice as old as all of them put together." – Mark Twain

"Come on," Ian shouted to me as we pushed our way through the crowd. "We don't want to be late for the ceremony."

"What ceremony?" I inquired breathlessly, struggling to keep up with him.

"You'll see soon enough," he replied. "First, we have to get to the river."

We pushed past throngs of Indian pilgrims until the crowds slowed and finally stopped just short of the Ganges River. In the cool of late evening, hundreds of people stood watching the brightly-lit ceremony that was taking place on one of the main stone piers along the river. Ian told me that these piers were called Ghats, and stretch along the western side of the Ganges. All of them have steps that lead directly into the water.

Priests dressed in white robes stood on wooden platforms

The Ghats of Varanasi on the banks of the Ganges

The streets of Varanasi

facing the river. As they chanted mantras together, bare-chested attendants below them beat drums and crashed cymbals. The priests held lighted candles towards the darkened river as the young attendants rang bells in unison. The crowd watched the scene in reverential silence.

"This is called the Aarti ceremony," whispered Ian. "It happens here every evening at this time. The priests give devotions to Mother Ganges or Ganga Ma, as they call the river. The Ganges is very important to Indian Hindus. Most important ceremonies take place on the Ghats, they are the heart and soul of Varanasi," he said, with a clenched fist for dramatic effect.

After the ceremony had finished, Ian bought a lotus leaf and a small candle for us both. He placed the lighted candle on the lotus leaf and pushed them off to join the countless other flickering flames on the water. I followed his lead and did likewise. It was a lovely sight, a great flotilla of flames gently floating on the holy river. All along the Ghats, pilgrims and tourists were doing the same thing. As people chanted and beat drums around us, it was easy to see that Varanasi was a special city.

Varanasi was the ideal choice for my first stop in India. Located in the north of the country, it is one of the holiest and most interesting cities in the subcontinent. I felt that it would be an ideal place to get my introduction to this fascinating and colourful land. I had left my other travelling companions behind in Nepal to catch a flight to India. It was on the flight from Kathmandu to Varanasi that I had met Ian and we had shared a taxi from the airport to the city. Ian was from Liverpool and had visited Varanasi the previous year so he knew his way around. He had studied yoga in India for a year and was returning to continue his studies.

After the ceremony, I realised that I hadn't eaten since breakfast. Ian suggested a restaurant nearby that he had eaten at before. The place was a very simple affair with walls of peeling paint and bare steel tables and chairs. I was too hungry to be bothered about the décor. Some Indian customers paused from their meal to stare at us as we sat at a table. I noticed that they didn't use knives or forks, preferring instead to eat with their fingers. The menu contained a bewildering list of dishes that I had never heard of before. Ian volunteered to select some courses for the both of us and I was happy to let him do so.

Twenty minutes later, two waiters appeared with plates of delicious looking food. I first had a masala dosa, which is a crispy pancake filled with a scrumptious mixture of spiced tomato sauce and vegetables. This was followed by a dish called thali, a smorgasbord of colourful and wonderful tasting dips and sauces, surrounding a heap of boiled rice. There was also dal (lentil puree), vegetable curry, and a cooling yogurt called raita. Wheels of roti bread accompanied all this terrific food. The waiter placed a fork and knife in front of us but Ian ignored the cutlery and dived into the food with his fingers. I followed his lead and I was soon relishing the new experience of eating food with my fingers. I couldn't keep from commenting between each mouthful how good the food was. Best of all, the waiter came round to our table every few minutes and topped-up any of the dishes that we liked.

After the meal, Ian organised a taxi to take him to the train station. He was anxious to be at the ashram for his yogi studies the following day. I thanked him for his help and waved him off as he sped away in the taxi. It was my great luck to have met Ian, as he was a huge help to me in finding me feet during my first day in chaotic and busy India.

I wandered through the narrow lanes of old Varanasi towards my guesthouse. As I did, a man emerged from the shadows and started walking with me.

"Sir, you want hash, marijuana, or opium? I have good stuff, it make you fly, fly high in the sky. No problem. Good price," He whispered, all in one breath. He had bad black teeth and wore a cheap, ill-fitting, grey suit. His eyes looked watery and bloodshot and he staggered slightly as he walked with me. I waved a hand in refusal and quickened my pace to the guesthouse.

Before we had rushed off to see the Aarti Ceremony, Ian had also helped me to find a place to stay. Modern Vision Guesthouse had basic rooms arranged in three levels around a small courtyard, which gave the impression of being a prison block. I walked up the three flights of concrete stairs to my solitary cell. The room was sparse with a cold concrete floor and no hot water. I dawdled on the landing outside my room for a while and listened to the bolts slide in each door as people retired for the night. I tried to read for a while by the dim light bulb before admitting defeat and turning in.

It was destined to be a fitful night's sleep. The pillow was dirty and mosquitoes feasted on me during the night. I heard scuttling sounds around the room during the dead of night and something made a good attempt at eating through my backpack on the concrete floor. The sounds of fireworks, drums, wailing cats, and fighting dogs all combined to keep me awake throughout the night.

Dawn is said to be the best time to see the Ganges and I was up early the following morning to take a boat trip on the river. So early in fact, that the guesthouse owner was not yet awake and I had to rouse him so he could unlock the front door and let me out. It was still not yet light as I walked along the Ghats. The water that lapped gently along the stone embankments was choked with huge amounts of raw sewage and rubbish. Human waste and urine peppered the ground as people, cows, and dogs use the Ghats to relieve themselves.

Soon, a man approached me and offered to take me out on the river. We agreed on a price and I was soon aboard a wooden rowing boat, moving through the Ganges in the dim light of early morning. Even then, the river was busy as pilgrims and tourists traversed its waters. The Ghats themselves seemed to glow with a dull, reddish hue in the early morning light. All along the river, people were bathing, washing, and offering devotions to Mother Ganges. I watched as a Hindu holy man called a *Sadu* waded into the water up to his waist to offer his devotions in the river. He was bare-chested and his hair was matted with thick dreadlocks, which fell down over his tanned face. With his thin hands joined together, he immersed himself completely in the river before coming up again. With water dripping freely from his body, he shut his eyes tight to the world as his lips trembled with unheard prayers. I watched him repeat his devotions until he disappeared from view.

We rowed south along the river, past the remains of the red brick palaces and mansions that had been built by the city's royalty. Bushes and small trees now sprouted from the ruined turrets of the formerly grand homes. The boatman pointed at the walls of the palace.

"You see that dark line on the wall? Heavy Monsoon rains caused the Ganges to flood in 1984. That line marks the height of the waters." The watermark was over halfway up the walls of the palace. At that height, most of the city must have been inundated.

The boatman slowed beside a Ghat where a large fire was burning. According to my guidebook, this was Harishchandra, one of the oldest Ghats in Varanasi. This was where the bodies of the dead were cremated on large pyres of wood. Within the orange flames, I could make out a human shape as the relentless flames consumed it. The boatman pointed to the building behind the fire.

"That building is an electric crematorium. Some people cannot afford to pay for the expensive sandalwood required for the fire but, for three hundred rupees (about six euros), they can burn the body there."

The boatman leaned closer to me.

"Would you like me to go closer?" he asked.

"No, thanks," I replied. I felt I would have plenty of time to see death during my coming days in Varanasi.

As we rowed away from the burning Ghat, I looked back at the blackish smoke that rose from the funeral pyre. Both rich and poor were cremated on the same burning Ghats. Who could tell if the burning figure on the pyre was rich or poor? Who could discern if the ashes of the dead that lay at the bottom of the river were from the highest or lowest caste? Perhaps they attained the equality in death that they had been denied in life.

The boatman turned and rowed northwards towards some important Hindu temples. Another boat filled with Buddhist monks rowed alongside us for a while. Buddhists also consider Varanasi a holy city. I watched as their boat was intercepted by another vessel, laden down with bright orange flowers, candles, and other religious items for sale. It seemed that even on the river, there is no escape for the unrelenting vendors. Yet another boat pulled alongside them with the words 'Super Market' marked on its side and seemingly offering the contents of a real supermarket for sale. Up to then, the sun had been a pale disc in the murky fog but it finally rose to take its majestic place high in the morning sky and set the Ganges on fire.

Just as we turned for shore, I spotted a body floating in the water. It was partly decomposed and covered in white cloth that had started to peel off. Only metres away, people drank, bathed, and brushed their teeth with the same water. Death was truly part of life in Varanasi.

After my sleepless night at the Modern Vision Guesthouse, I decided to find somewhere better to stay. I located the perfect spot only a short distance away. Om Guesthouse was able to offer me a clean room with hot water and a television, which was all I needed. Once I settled in, I inquired at the front desk about somewhere to get breakfast, and was directed to a nearby restaurant called Baba's.

Baba's was a small restaurant on the roof of the building next to Om Guesthouse. I had to negotiate six flights of steep steps on the way to the roof and was breathless when I finally sat myself at a table. After a while, the manager appeared to take my order. He was an unusual looking character. He had narrow eyes, large protruding ears, and jagged bad teeth. His heavily greased black hair was combed straight back and he spoke with a slight lisp. As I was to discover, he was a very inquisitive man. When I told him I worked in the computer software industry, he asked me all manner of questions about computers and their inner workings. He spoke about the days before e-mail and telephones, when the Muslim people used to send messages via carrier pigeons. During a pause in his ramblings, I managed to order an Indian breakfast. It consisted of yogurt-like buffalo curd, sweet milky India tea called chai, and a selection of vegetable sauces with four puffed puri breads. It was delicious, cheap, and a breakfast that I was to enjoy every morning during my time in Varanasi.

Baba asked me how I found India so far and I told him that I thought India was a great country. He shook his head in disagreement.

"Things were better when the Britishers ruled India, Mr. John," he confided. "India is dirty, corrupt, poor, and uneducated. The Britishers knew how to run this country," he said, raising both his arms as if holding an imaginary rifle.

"Well," I answered, "India is no longer under British rule. Ghandi helped to get rid of the British. He must be a great hero in India." Incredibly, he disagreed.

"I do not like Mr. Ghandi. He forced the Britishers to leave too soon. India would not be divided if he had not forced them to leave."

He leaned closer to me.

"Mr. John, in my heart, I would welcome the Britishers back again," he admitted, imaging that this would cure all of India's problems. "And the Irish too," he added politely after a short pause.

The restaurant had a great view of the Ganges and of the countless flat roofs of the city. From my vantage point, I watched people hanging out their washing to dry on the roofs of their homes. In the distance, boats criss-crossed the route between the Ghats and the unoccupied far shore. On a roof below me, two monkeys were trying to take a television antenna apart. One climbed to the top of the antenna, shaking it violently, while the other attempted to eat through the cable leading from it. I hoped the owners weren't watching anything important.

It had been a hectic introduction to India so, once I finished my breakfast at Baba's, I returned to the comforts of Om Guesthouse to catch up on some reading. I also watched *Terminator 2: Judgement Day* on the television but the power kept cutting out just as Arnold was about to wreak havoc on some unsuspecting victims. At some stage, I drifted off to sleep and awoke some hours later. I checked my watch to discover that it was seven that evening. I had recovered some of the sleep lost to the Modern Vision Guesthouse. Pangs of hunger forced me to leave the room and return to Baba's for supper.

Baba smiled when he saw me and wasted little time in telling me about his latest acquisition.

"Mr. John, you know this Steve Austin?" he inquired. "I have recently acquired cable television and had the opportunity to watch this WWF wrestling last night." He laughed as he recounted the muscles of some of the wrestlers.

"They are so strong and we Indians are so thin and weak, they would kill me with one blow," he said as he swiped the air with his fist in demonstration. "Some of them get one million American dollars for twenty minutes work." He cleaned off my table with a cloth but seemed lost in thought as he turned away.

"That is good business," he muttered to himself.

The restaurant had a mix of tourists and some locals. Two Indian girls sat at the table next to mine and I started talking with them. They told me they were studying for their business degrees at the local University. They spoke excellent English and seemed very educated. As we spoke, I broached the subject of arranged marriages in India and asked them their feelings on the subject. They surprised me when they both admitted that their parents had already arranged partners for them. I had assumed that the custom of arranged marriages only still persisted among rural people.

"We feel a bit sad about this," they admitted. "It is the wish of our parents and so, we much accept it."

"In the West, it would be very strange to be marrying someone that you had never met," I said. They nodded in agreement.

"Yes, this must be strange for you. There are some love marriages in India but usually only in the big cities."

"But surely you would like to choose your husband instead of having him chosen for you," I asked. They shook their heads in disagreement.

"Who has our best interests at heart but our parents? Who will put all their experience of life into choosing a good man for us? Our parents want us to have happy marriages and will choose the best partner for us."

They saw the look of disbelief on my face.

"It is not so bad. We do get to spend some time with our prospective husbands before we must tell our parents if we like them or not," they explained. That wasn't so bad, I thought. At least they could get to know each other first. I asked how much time they got with their suitor.

"One or two hours," they explained casually.

After I finished supper at Baba's, I walked back towards my guesthouse. I had planned to get an early night but the sounds of the Ghats beckoned me back towards them again. I hadn't gone far when I heard a familiar voice.

"Sir, you want hash, marijuana, or opium?" The grey-suited weed dealer appeared from the shadows to again attempt to sell me his wares. I waved him away and moved on quickly. I treaded carefully in the darkness on my way towards the main burning Ghat of Manikarnika. This is the biggest burning Ghat in Varanasi. Even from a distance, the flames from the multitude of burning pyres lit up the night. Once I reached the Ghat, I stood a respectful distance away and observed the scene before me.

"Please, no photos," whispered the voice. A thin looking man had positioned himself beside me. "I can explain about the burning Ghat if you wish," he said, and was into his routine before I could stop him.

"Please, come closer," he said as he beckoned me to follow him nearer to the fires. He brought me to the railing that surrounded the main funeral pyres. I could feel the heat of the flames on my face as they engulfed body after body.

"When people die in Varanasi, they are happy as it breaks the cycle of birth, death and rebirth, what we call Samsara," said my guide. "When the cycle is broken, there is no more suffering for the souls. This is a very holy place for Indian people."

As he spoke, a brass band passed by in full flow, heralding what I expected would be a wedding party. That was until I saw the pallbearers carrying a body following behind them. It seemed that death in Varanasi was a cause for celebration. The light of the fires danced on the faces of the people watching. Other corpses, dressed in fine silks with richly woven designs, waited their turn. I watched as orange flames engulfed the blackened human shape that was jammed between logs of sandalwood.

"Five kinds of people cannot be cremated at the burning Ghat," my guide continued. "Children under five years, pregnant women, holy men, snake bite victims, and lepers."

"What happens to those people then?" I asked.

"A stone is tried to them and they are thrown into the river," he said. The body I had seen in the water that morning must have been one of these people.

The guide explained that it takes about two hundred and fifty kilos of wood to burn a body in about three hours. The flame that lights each pyre never goes out and is said to be eternal. Women are wrapped in gold cloth, while men are wrapped in white before going into the fire.

It was hellish scene of death. One flaming pyre contained a bandaged and bloody figure, whose upper body and arms were thrust upwards, as if trying to sit up. On the pyre next to that, only a blackened skull was visible, as the flames had consumed the rest of the body. A popping sound from the fire behind me signalled a head exploding in the heat as other organs sizzled. At the river's edge below the fires, young children sifted through the ashes of the dead, hoping to find a ring or gold filling left behind by the flames. The smell of burning flesh filled the air. I walked away quickly from that place with a feeling of dread in my stomach.

The guide showed me the special area where only the dead of the Brahmin, the highest caste, were cremated.

"However," he said, "the monsoon sometimes causes the river to rise very high and cover all the burning areas so everyone, high and low caste, must be cremated on the roof."

I watched some people shovel the ashes of the dead into the river. He noticed my gaze.

"Those people are Doms, the untouchables," my guide explained. "It is their job to work in the burning Ghat." I had heard that this can be a well-paid position and can be passed down from father to son for generations.

"Two hundred and twenty bodies can be burned here in twenty four hours. The cost is two thousand rupees per body."

"Two thousand rupees is a small fortune in India," I said aloud.

"Yes, is a lot of money but people can help with the cost," he suggested.

He then explained that he worked on behalf of the poor people who lived in the building just behind the burning Ghat. They were waiting to die and couldn't afford the cost of the expensive sandalwood needed for the cremation. I thought this was terrible at first – imagine a retirement home overlooking a graveyard. However, I started to think that maybe these people looked forward to the day of their death with joy. Finally, their soul could break free of this world of pain and suffering.

I didn't know whether to believe his story until he brought me into one of these buildings. The place seemed overcrowded and elderly people squatted down along the walls in silence. While we were there, a young shaven-headed boy, sobbing with tears, was ushered past us.

"Crying is not allowed at the fire," explained the guide sadly. "It impedes the passage of the soul."

I asked why the boy had a shaved head.

"He is the eldest son and chief mourner so according to our traditions, he must shave his head. It is also his job to light the pyre that consumes the body."

I donated some money to the home and thanked the guide for his help. Of course, he insisted on a donation also. In Varanasi, such public cremations seem to be a very ordinary and natural thing. The burning of the bodies didn't seem grotesque or obscene, but was done with respect and reverence. Ashes to ashes, dust to dust. As I passed the fires, the wind changed suddenly and the acrid stench of burning flesh engulfed my nostrils. I covered my mouth and nose with my hand. I had enough of death for one day.

ॐ

I left the guesthouse early the following morning with no particular destination in mind. As usual, the Ghats were a hive of activity. Kids played cricket with narrow planks of wood and a rubber ball. Women washed clothes by beating them on the steps of the Ghats. Nearby, a man washed his cattle in the water as the remainder of the herd rested in the morning sun, nonchalantly swatting flies with their tails as they contentedly chewed the cud.

I left the Ghats behind and emerged in one of Varanasi's main streets. It was a chaotic scene of honking cars, motorbikes, and rickshaws. Cows wandered the busy street as men passed them pulling carts laden with goods. I noticed that the ground was stained red with what I first thought was blood. I later discovered that this was in fact a concoction called betel nut, a mixture of the areca nut and betel leaf. The people chew this mixture for pleasure, as it is mildly intoxicating.

I left the bedlam of the main street, and went looking for a Hindu temple that had been mentioned in my guidebook. I eventually found the temple and, as I approached it, I got my first sight of real Indian poverty. About thirty people had formed a small settlement outside the temple walls. They used plastic sheeting suspended with wooden stakes for shelter, and cooked over open, smoky fires. Nearby, people joined street dogs as they picked through a mountain of reeking rubbish, searching for anything that could be used or eaten. Naked children played next to open sewers. I turned and walked back in the direction I had come from. I had lost interest in seeing the temple. Poverty such as this was, unfortunately, a common scene in Varanasi.

ॐ

I looked forward to each visit to Baba's, not only for the good food, but also for the entertainment provided by its manager. I returned there that evening for supper. Once I had ordered, Baba told me that he had been watching a lot of WWF wrestling on cable television. He spoke very animatedly about how his hero, John Stepson, had been defeated by two fighters in the ring the night before. He also mentioned a wrestler called The Rhino and waxed lyrical about his great strength and physique. He told me that watching all that wrestling had inspired him with a brilliant business idea. He wanted me to join him in starting the WWI, World Wrestling India. I tried to stop myself from bursting out laughing as he detailed his proposed stable of wrestlers.

Once I managed to convince Baba that I had no interest in setting up a wrestling franchise in India, I returned to my meal.

"Man, that wrestling idea was great. You should have gone for it," said the man at the next table, as he rocked with laughter. Andre was South African and had been in India for nearly a year. He was thin looking and deeply tanned. He had a head of thick dreadlocks tied back with a bright headband and wore a light but colourful top. He had the musky scent of the travelling hippie, and spoke in a low voice.

We talked for a while about our impressions of India.

"God, I'd murder a cold beer right now," I said. The Ganges

is considered so holy that alcohol is banned within one mile of it.

Andre moved closer to me and smiled. "I know just the place," he whispered.

He led the way across the darkened Ghats to the Shanti Guesthouse. Shanti seemed like a party place where dread-locked Israelis smoked weed along with groups of giggling girls. Others just sat by themselves and stared into space. We ordered a beer and sat with a French guy that Andre knew. He'd been to India a number of times he told me that he always preferred to stay in one place for a long period of time. He spent an hour talking about how horrible life in the West was and how 'free' he felt now. I suppose he had a point. A Westerner traveller is as free as anyone is ever likely to be. There's no job to worry about, no family to care for, and no responsibilities to tie you down. You can come and go as you please.

I didn't like Shanti but I still ordered another beer, which tasted terrible. The bottle was labelled Premium Australian Lager, so I guess that was about right. Andre kept fidgeting and couldn't relax. A joint was being passed around and was offered to Andre.

"I'm off the gear man, no more for me," he said, waving the joint away. "I've smoked enough weed to last me a lifetime." Eventually, he could take no more.

"Let's get the hell out of here, man," he said to me in an urgent voice. "All this weed smoke is killing me. I'm trying to give it up." We finished our beers and headed into the night. We parted company at the bottom of the steps to Shanti. The last I saw of him, he was talking very animatedly to the weed dealer with the grey suit.

The next morning, I climbed those steep steps to Baba's one last time. Over my Indian breakfast, I watched the boats taking pilgrims and tourists on the Ganges. Other travellers were eating breakfast on rooftops below me and admiring the morning scenery just as I was doing. The monkeys were already screeching on the rooftops and causing havoc. One of them was jumping up and down on a corrugated roof, seemingly with no reason other than to cause the biggest racket he could.

Baba sat with me for a while as I ate breakfast. He mentioned in passing that he could make any passport I wished for four thousand rupees. He saw my hesitation and quickly dropped his price to two thousand. The idea intrigued me. I've always fancied having a few extra passports in my bag, just in case I ever need to make a quick getaway. I smiled at the thought of the various identities I could have – one with a ridiculous fake moustache and wig, and another with a patch over my left eye. As appealing at it was, I refused his offer. I took a few photos of Baba and the staff and returned to my room to finish packing.

In Varanasi, death is part of everyday life. It's in the flames, the river and the air you breathe. It is something that the people embrace as an inevitable part of the journey of life. The fact is we will all die and in Varanasi, you are reminded about this at every turn.

Once I collected my bags, I hailed a rickshaw. It was time for me to say goodbye to the Ghats. As I climbed into the rickshaw, a hand tapped me on the shoulder.

"You want hash, weed, opium, good prices..." His voice trailed away as the rickshaw pulled off and headed for the train station.

15

THE JEWEL OF INDIA

Whitened bones spilled from the young woman's bag and scattered across the floor. They were large and unmistakably human. Everyone in the waiting hall stopped what they were doing to stare at the woman as she scrambled to gather them up. I leaned down and picked up what looked like a large femur bone that had landed close to my feet. I handed it back to the young woman without a word. My face must have registered a thousand questions. She looked at me and smiled awkwardly.

"For my medical studies," she said, as she hurried back to her seat. That incident was easily the most exciting thing to have happened that evening as I waited in Varanasi station for the train to Agra. I shared the small waiting room with about a dozen other restless passengers. The train had already been delayed by four hours. The young woman with the bag of bones told me that, like her friends with her, she was a medical student returning to Rajasthan for a holiday after their exams. They were full of questions about life in Ireland, a country that they knew little about. They asked how old I was and found it very

The Taj Mahal

surprising that I wasn't married at the age of thirty two.

"All Indian people of your age are married with children," explained one of them. "It is normal in India."

"Do young people not want to stay single until they're older?" I asked them. They all shook their heads.

"No. We want to marry as soon as we are finished our studies."

I found that this was the prevailing attitude in India, although it was changing. Traditionally, young people sought marriage and a family at an early age. With India's increasing economic growth and prosperity, it would not be long before more people waited longer before settling down.

Ten hours after I arrived at the station, crackling speakers announced the imminent arrival of the train to Agra. Everyone quickly gathered their belongings and headed for the platform. As soon as the train came to a halt, there was an almighty dash for the doors. People were tired and there were a few heated exchanges in the crush. Once inside, I found that the carriage was in total darkness and I had trouble locating my berth. I moved along the crowded and darkened passage slowly, trying to make out the berth numbers. In desperation, I started to shout out my bunk number.

"Twenty seven, that's across from me mate," came an English accident from the darkness. With great relief, I stowed my backpack, climbed onto my upper bunk, and introduced myself. Nick was a Londoner and had been travelling around India for the previous three months. He was also an avid photographer told me that this passion meant carrying a large amount of professional equipment on his travels. Along with camera bodies, lenses, a tripod, and carrying case, he carried a laptop to edit the digital pictures. It must have been quiet a burden.

There was no pillow or blanket on my bunk and I had to make do with a thin mattress to sleep on. I used my daypack as a pillow and threw a few t-shirts over me for warmth. Not the most comfortable but it had to do. I soon curled up into the foetal position and tried to sleep.

I awoke the next morning not feeling the best. I had a minor stomach problem in Varanasi before I left and it had gotten worse. Stomach cramps caused me to curl up in pain and I felt very weak. I broke out in cold sweats every so often and felt like passing out. All I could do was lie on my bunk and stare at the ceiling. Nick was great and insisted that I try to eat some plain rice to help me regain my strength. I managed to eat some and felt a little better afterwards. The medical students also came by and when they discovered that I was ill, they argued heatedly about what my symptoms might mean, and everything from malaria to the common cold was suggested as a possible diagnosis. As we neared our destination, I started to feel better and managed to drink more water.

We arrived in Agra the following evening after a train journey that had lasted almost twenty-four hours. Nick and I got a taxi to bring us to the Sheela Hotel, located close to the entrance of the Taj Mahal. This would be a perfect base for my planned visit to the world famous symbol of India. At the Sheela hotel, the manager informed us that there were no showers available but we could get a bucket of hot water if we needed to wash. I readily accepted the bucket and waited at reception to collect it. While I was there, I met some other travellers who complained bitterly that the Taj Mahal had been barely visible through the heavy fog that had shrouded the city that day. Fog in December is common in Agra. This news worried me a little, but I hoped that it would have cleared by the following morning. Once I had availed of my bucket shower, Nick and I went in search of food.

We walked through the city's dirty and seedy streets as bikes and rickshaws flew by. As we rounded a corner, we came across an Indian wedding procession. It was a spectacular sight. The richly decorated groom, mounted on a white horse, headed the dazzling and colourful procession. The wedding carriage followed close behind him and was drawn by two other white horses, each decorated with tall red headdresses. The wedding carriage itself was festooned with flashing lights and looked like something from a fairy tale. The shy but bejewelled bride peeked out from inside the carriage. About ten women followed the carriage, each one carrying an electrified chandelier on her head. Each chandelier was connected to the one behind with a thick electric cable. The electricity was provided by a sparking generator, which sat on a rickshaw and was pushed along by its sweating owner. The wedding party danced crazily and let off firecrackers as they went by.

We eventually found a restaurant and sat down to order a meal. Most Indian restaurants don't serve alcohol but, if you ask nicely, you may be in luck. When the waiter took our order, I beckoned him closer.

"Is it possible to get some beer?" I whispered, my eyes looking trustingly into his.

"Yes, it is possible," he replied quietly and withdrew from our table. He returned some time later with our food and a teapot. I waited patiently for the beer to arrive but, after twenty minutes, there was still no sign of it. I called the waiter over once again.

"Can you bring the beer now please?" I asked, resting my hand on his forearm and using my most pleading tone. He nodded to the teapot, tapped it with his finger, and left us without a word. I poured from the teapot to discover pale beer filling up my cup. As Ian and I enjoyed cup after cup of 'tea', I couldn't help but worry about the fog. I only had one day in Agra and I would only get one chance to see the Taj Mahal, fog or no fog.

My heart sank when I drew back the curtains in my room the following morning. The city remained hidden behind a blanket of thick fog. Nick and I walked down to the river and we could barely see ten feet in front of us, never mind the Taj. We trudged back to the hotel dejectedly and decided to wait it out, hoping the fog would clear by the afternoon.

As we walked back, Nick seemed to be particularly despondent. He told me how it had always been his dream to photograph the Taj Mahal.

"I've taken some good photographs throughout India but the one I've always dreamed about is a photo of the Taj Mahal with a camel." He said, his eyes almost misting up. "That would combine the two beautiful images of India into one. It wouldn't be hard to sell that photo."

By eleven that morning, there had only been a small improvement in the weather. I wondered how long I was willing to wait for the fog to clear. I didn't want to waste a whole day sitting in the hotel, staring into the white blankness outside. I had enjoyed a great run of luck with the sites along my route so I couldn't complain if one got away. Just as I was about to give up, the sun suddenly broke through and gradually, the fog lifted. I didn't know how long it would stay that way so Nick and I hurried to the entrance of the Taj Mahal.

The stone gate framed the Taj beautifully as we entered the complex. Nick was as excited as a child on Christmas morning. The Taj is the splendid mausoleum built by the Emperor Shah Jahan for his second wife. It took twenty-two years to complete and involved over twenty thousand workers and artisans from as far away as Italy. As Ian snapped photographs happily, I walked to the long pool, where the reflection of the Taj's onion-shaped dome shimmered gently in the water. I stood and admired the perfect symmetry of the building with a minaret on each corner. I then joined the hordes that flowed down along the sides of the pool and into the Taj itself. Two mosques sit either side of the main building but one is purely ornamental, as it doesn't face Mecca. I removed my shoes before entering the Taj.

Inside, the internal walls were studded with precious stone inlay and incredibly intricate designs. Replicas of the tombs of the Emperor Shah Jahan and his beloved wife lay behind a screen, but the real tombs are locked in the basement and not open to the public. There were so many people crushed inside the Taj that it became uncomfortable so I left to look for Nick. I found him sweating heavily under the weight of his camera gear but happy with his day.

It would take several days to appreciate all the marvels that the Taj has to offer but I was more than contented with one. We decided we had had enough of the crowds and wandered towards the Jammu River that runs behind the Taj. There, we were able to take a boat across to the opposite bank. As we crossed, I turned back to see the Taj silhouetted beautifully against the setting sun. Nick clicked away happily, muttering his satisfaction from time to time. As we neared the opposite bank, I saw a camel coming towards us with a young rider on its back. I tapped Nick on the shoulder.

"Nick," I said, "Get ready to be happy."

When he saw the camel, Nick whooped with joy. As we got ashore, Nick rushed towards the camel owner and rashly started promising him all sorts of money for photographs. He was soon positioning both camel and rider in front of the Taj for a photo session. Touts appeared from nowhere selling postcards and chessboards. In India, there is no escape from the omnipresent tout. Eventually, the sun turned into an orange ball as it set behind the Taj and our day ended. We caught the boat back across the river and trudged contentedly back to the hotel.

Nick and I exchanged contact details the next morning as we went our separate ways. I caught a taxi to Agra train station to get one of the frequent trains to Delhi. The station contained many shops that sold a wide range of items for the traveller. Pillows, blankets, books, magazines, and toys were all available. Waiting passengers could also avail of a basic hostel at the station while they waited between long train connections. A number of very good vegetarian restaurants provided cheap and filling meals. Train stations in India are almost like self-contained towns, with everything the traveller might need.

I waited patiently in the queue to buy my ticket but others pushed ahead of me. An Indian ticket queue is no place for manners so I pushed and shoved until I got my ticket. As I waited at the platform for the train, a cow meandered by, nonchalantly chewing the cud and swinging it tail with abandon, scattering some waiting passengers.

"Only in India," I thought.

The train arrived on time and I took my seat next in the crowded carriage. It wasn't long before I was talking with the Indian man seated next to me. Like China, I found there was never a shortage of friendly people in train stations. Once I told him where I was from, he asked me to explain the situation in Northern Ireland, which he confessed had puzzled him. I tried my best and in turn, I asked him about the situation in Kashmir. I think we only succeeded in confusing each other.

As I stared out the train window, I saw some children flying kites in a small park. My neighbour noticed me watching.

"These are fighting kites, not for playing," he explained. "The string near the kite has sharpened glass and can cut the other kite." He demonstrated by lifting his hands in the air, mimicking two kites meeting in flight. "One is cut and falls to the ground," he explained, his hand hitting the small table with a thud. "The winner keeps the fallen kite."

The train travelled very slowly and we arrived in Delhi an hour later than scheduled but that's India for you. In my short time in the country, I could see that you needed a very flexible itinerary if you wanted to enjoy the country. Sticking to a rigid timetable would only lead to frustration. After I left the train, I got an auto-rickshaw to Pahar Ganj, the backpacker area of Delhi where many of the budget hotels and guesthouses are located.

Pahar Ganj was an ugly looking place, with narrow streets, high buildings, and congested traffic. I jumped out of the rickshaw and walked along the busy thoroughfare, people bumping into me all the way. The street was badly potholed and strewn with rubbish. Tacky shops selling silk scarves shared the street with small restaurants and guesthouses. I popped into the first hotel I saw and was glad I did. They showed me a lovely room that had an en-suite bathroom, a large bed, and cable television. I took it and settled into my new room. It felt nice to splash out on a bit of luxury, especially in India.

As soon as I left the hotel to go for food, a rickshaw emerged from the crowd and cut out in front of me.

"Sir, where are you going now?" asked the driver. He wore a dirty cloth wrap around his head and his teeth were blackened with decay. His eyes were blood-shot and heavy. I tried to step around him but he cleverly played on my sense of fairness.

"Sir, sir, why are you so rude? How have I offended you?" I turned back to him to explain myself, but all he did was point me towards the back of the rickshaw. I realised this was just another ruse and walked on with his words of protestation ringing in my ears. From then on, every time I emerged from the hotel, the rickshaw driver would pounce on me and ask me the same question, "Sir, where are you going now?"

Over the next two days, I wandered around the sights of Delhi as if I were in a stupor. I visited the Red Fort, a popular tourist attraction in Old Delhi. The large walled citadel was built by Shah Jahan, the same man who had built the Taj Mahal. I wandered about its gardens and buildings but wasn't impressed. After seeing the Taj, nothing else could compare to it. It was a pity that this building had a hard act to follow as it was impressive in its own right. I left the Red Fort and caught a rickshaw to Jami Masjid, the biggest mosque in India. When I got there, I discovered that since it was Friday, it was closed to all non-Muslims. After that, I gave up on sightseeing and caught a rickshaw back to the hotel. I felt weary and tired. It wasn't that the city of Delhi wasn't interesting. My mind was elsewhere. I was already looking forward to seeing my family again at Christmas. I looked forward to meeting my friends in the local pub and telling them about my travels. I looked forward to sleeping in my own bed again. After ten weeks of travel, I had seen some incredible sights and met some fantastic people. I was ready to go home.

As I packed that night, I leafed through some of the pages of my journal. I felt that I had been travelling much longer than ten weeks. My journey had brought me through such fabled cities as Beijing, Shanghai, Lhasa, Kathmandu, and Varanasi. I had journeyed on the mighty Yangtze River and seen the sacred Ganges. I had journeyed deep into the majestic peaks of the Himalayas and seen the awesome face of Mount Everest. I had felt the religious fervour of Buddhist and Hindu temples and holy places. I had drank and eaten with people from different lands and cultures. I was satisfied.

I ordered a taxi to bring me to the airport the following morning. It was the end of the trail for me but I was happy to be going home. As I walked across the road to my waiting taxi, the rickshaw driver was true to form and emerged to cut me off. I walked around him as he asked, "Sir, where are you going now?"

"Home," I said with a broad smile. "I'm going home."

About The Author

John Dwyer comes from the Beara Peninsula in West Cork, Ireland. He has also written *Gael Force Thirteen*, a collection of thirteen short stories. This is his first book about his travels. He currently lives in Cork with his wife Caroline.

If you'd like to see more photographs of my trip – in colour this time – please visit my web site:

http://www.highroadtotibet.com

The web site also contains a collection of video clips I took on the road. There's also a blog where you can leave your comments and feedback about the book. I look forward to hearing from you.

— John Dwyer

Made in the USA
Middletown, DE
07 December 2015